Power Up!

DIAMOND

EDITION

Power Up!
DIAMOND
EDITION

Devotional Thoughts for BASEBALL FANS

DAVE BRANON, EDITOR

DISCOVERY HOUSE
PUBLISHERS®

Feeding the Soul with the Word of God

Discovery House Publishers is affiliated with RBC Ministries,
Grand Rapids, Michigan.

Discovery House books are distributed to the trade exclusively by
Barbour Publishing, Inc., Uhrichsville, Ohio.

Interior design by Sherri L. Hoffman

ISBN: 978-1-57293-318-7

Printed in the United States of America

09 10 11 12 /   / 10 9 8 7 6 5 4 3 2 1

CONTENTS

INTRODUCTION

The one constant through all the years, Ray," intones James Earl Jones as Terence Mann in *Field of Dreams*, "has been **baseball**."

I love the way Jones interpreted that single noun—*baseball*—as he made his heartfelt Mann-plea, trying to convince Ray Kinsella not to sell his carved-out-of-corn baseball field despite the threat of imminent bankruptcy. Jones/Mann spoke it with a reverent singularity, endowing it with an importance appreciated by all who love the game.

"America," Mann continues, "has rolled by like an army of steamrollers, and erased like a blackboard, rebuilt, and erased again. But **baseball** has marked the time. This field, this game. It's a part of our past. It reminds us of all that once was good and that could be again. Ahhh, people will come, Ray. People will most definitely come."

Baseball. For so many, it is a word of comfort, a representation of joy, a reminder of summer days and American heroes.

Baseball has accompanied a country for 150 years on its long march to superiority—always there in its plateaus and valleys. Through wars and rumors of wars, it has been present as a beacon of familiarity and hopefulness and new beginnings.

Baseball has spawned cultural icons with magical names like Babe Ruth. Ty Cobb. Jackie Robinson. Willie Mays. Mickey Mantle. Hank Aaron. Pete Rose.

Baseball has been marked by controversies: the Black Sox, strikes, and steroids.

Baseball has given us some of the most remarkable venues in American sports architecture: Yankee Stadium. Wrigley Field. Fenway Park. Dodger Stadium. Camden Yards.

Baseball has punctuated our lives with memorable moments that threaten to nudge aside even the top images of a nation's history for their dramatic appeal: Bobby Thomson's home run, Don Larsen's perfect game, Bill Mazeroski's surprising World Series winner, Kirk Gibson's miracle shot, Carlton Fisk's body English blast, Joe Carter's Fall Classic walk off in Toronto.

Baseball. People most definitely come.

Seventy million of them each year hand over their money to sit in the sunshine of a summer's day or in the cool of an August evening and watch as baseball players live out their dreams on expanses of grass and dirt. They come because the game is as American as Abraham Lincoln. They come because even if the game doesn't have the collisions and the clashing helmets of football or the fast action of basketball or hockey, it has statistics, tradition, history, and a beauty unmatched by any other sport. They come because it is what Americans have done since 1869.

Baseball. The game gives you time to think, to contemplate, to embellish.

And baseball gives us an opportunity to tie its own stories, oddities, and narratives to a much more important area of pursuit: spiritual truth.

For the past several years, the writers of *Sports Spectrum* magazine's devotional guide *Power Up!* have used a number of sports to create analogies with which to point out biblical truth. Not surprisingly, the most popular sport these writers have employed to spin their articles has been baseball.

Baseball. Terence Mann said it "reminds us of all that once was good." Let's take that a step further. Let's use baseball to remind us of all that is godly. By using its stories, its people, its history, and its familiarity, we hope to introduce you to a wide range of principles from God's holy Word, the Bible.

Baseball. It's just one constant in this book. The other is so much more important, and that is the Bible. Speak that word with more reverence than even James Earl Jones could muster.

I am grateful that you "have most definitely come" to walk alongside us in this book as we use the great game of baseball to teach eternal, unchanging truths.

DAVE BRANON, EDITOR
Power Up! Diamond Edition

THE TOP 100 CHRISTIAN BASEBALL PLAYERS

One of the bonus features that we thought would enhance your enjoyment of this book is a list of the Top 100 Christian baseball players of all time. You will notice that with each devotional article we have included a short note about the player that corresponds with the number of the devotional—beginning with Christy Mathewson, who we have named the best Christian baseball player in the history of the game.

This was not an easy task.

Compiling a list of professed Christians and then comparing them with other believers goes against a standard I used during my 18 years as managing editor of *Sports Spectrum* magazine. Although we knew our readers wanted us to create such lists (they often asked for a list of all the Christians on the New York Yankees, for instance), we resisted the urge to compile such lists for several reasons.

For one, who on this side of heaven can really know who the truly born-again people are? Can any of us look inside a person's heart and know for sure that he or she has trusted Jesus Christ as Savior and Lord? That's just not possible for us as mere mortals. Plus, because we cannot be in every clubhouse and talk to every player, we have to depend on others to tell us who the fellow Christians are. Sometimes, we may miss a few for a variety of reasons. Listing Christians alone, then, presents its own problems.

Another reason this is tough is that we are attempting to go back into history and pinpoint players from eras before our time. Here we have to depend on what we have heard about people who may have died before we were even born, and with thousands upon thousands of names to consider, surely there are going to be people we missed.

Also, as we try to compile the list, do we put baseball players we have observed to be stronger, more dedicated Christians above better players who may have been at best nominal in their faith—or do we go just by what we perceived to be their relative value as athletes using stats and honors alone? For instance, where do you put Dave Dravecky, whose stats don't compare with guys who stayed around longer but who became a beacon of Christian hope and faith because of his battle with cancer and amputation? Does he go in the Top 10 because of his impact for Christ through his story, his books, and his ministry? Or do we depend solely on the stats, which drops him to a much lower status?

And what about the new, young players? Some say Josh Hamilton has the ability to be a Mickey Mantle-type player, and his spectacular showing in the 2008 Home Run Derby certainly showed him to be a notch above most sluggers. But with just two seasons under his belt when this book was published, could we move him into the Top 10 already?

And mentioning Hamilton brings up another difficulty in making such a list. Hamilton himself recognizes that his past drug problems leave him on the brink of destruction at any time if he takes his eyes off Jesus and begins to look longingly at the drugs that nearly destroyed him. Any time we spotlight Christians in this way—as a magazine such as *Sports Spectrum* does—we risk being embarrassed should one of them stumble and fall spiritually. And putting these guys in a book even further immortalizes their stories and opens the door to ridicule should they tumble out of fellowship with God.

Another tough thing about this list was not letting personal preference override statistical, empirical evidence. For instance, it was tough to get done with the list (which, by the way, longtime *Sports Spectrum* colleague and writer Rob Bentz assisted me with) and discover that some of my favorite baseball guys were not in the Top 100. Mike Maroth, for instance, who has been among the most cooperative pro athletes I've ever encountered, was edged out. And Pat Kelly, a great evangelist who led many to Christ before his early death in 2005 at age 61, didn't make the list. I'll always cherish the opportunity to visit with Pat at RBC Ministries and tell him, "I was so excited to discover that Leroy Kelly, my all-time favorite Cleveland Browns player, is your brother" (Also, Andre Thornton, No. 63, is Pat's brother-in-law.). And outstanding Christians such as Jeremy Affeldt and Sid Bream—so accessible and so dedicated to serving Jesus—didn't crack the Top 100. Sorry, friends. Stats are sometimes nasty companions.

So, in a sense, we present the Top 100 to you in this book with a little fear and trembling. But we also think it is worth the effort and the challenge. In one way it honors these men for their outstanding careers—many of whom have been enshrined in the Baseball Hall of Fame and others who will arrive in Cooperstown someday. In another way, it gives honor to whom honor is due. It reminds each of us of the value of living out our faith in whatever profession God has called us to participate. These men testified of their belief in Jesus Christ in a secular world that does not often look kindly on matters of faith. For that, at least, they deserve our respect.

If we have erred in these selections by leaving someone out who should be here or by including someone who for some reason you feel should not have made the list, please forgive any perceived mistakes. It's an imperfect list compiled by imperfect people.

As someone whose love of baseball is among my very first memories of life—how I wish I could have included some of my favorite Cincinnati Reds on this list—let me invite you to enjoy reading through these names and the stories behind their inclusion. Any such list is a good discussion starter, and if creating this one starts some discussions about faith and Jesus and His role in our lives, then the effort was worthwhile.

—DAVE BRANON

1. SPRING TRAINING: BACK TO BASICS

"Add to your faith goodness; and to goodness, knowledge."
2 PETER 1:5

Nothing warms the heart of a snowbound northerner quite like these February words: "Pitchers and catchers report on Friday." Hallelujah! The winter of our discontent is nearly over.

But does spring training really matter? Sure, it's fun, but why do players run wind sprints in the outfield *during the game*?

According to veteran major league manager Lou Piniella, spring training matters a lot. "We have 18 instructors in camp because we need every one of them," he said.

FAST FACT:
The major league record for Opening Day starts by a pitcher is 16 by Hall of Fame pitcher Tom Seaver.

So, Piniella's players spend tons of time in the spring working on the fundamentals and honing the little things that make a big difference.

"We tend to take these intricate ballets for granted in the summer because they seem so habitual," says author and baseball fan William Zinsser of major league baseball games. "Spring training efforts in March pay off in August."

The same principle holds true in our spiritual fitness. Second Peter 1:5–7 outlines the basics of an all-star quality faith. We start with the most fundamental building block—faith in Jesus Christ. To that we add goodness—doing what is right in every circumstance. Then, by reading the Bible, we gain spiritual knowledge. To knowledge we add self-control, which comes from the Holy Spirit who dwells in each follower of Jesus. Self-control needs perseverance, to which we add godliness (becoming like Jesus). Godliness leads to brotherly kindness, and brotherly kindness is made complete in love. One basic placed on top of another until we are ready for action.

Peter told us, "If you possess these qualities in increasing measure, they will keep you from being ineffective and unproductive in your knowledge of our Lord Jesus Christ" (v. 8). It's time to report for training.

—TIM GUSTAFSON

FOLLOW THROUGH

Do you spend any time on the "spiritual fundamentals"? How often do you read God's instruction manual, the Bible? How often do you pray? Consider making a list of prayer requests and praises, and praying through them each morning.

From the Playbook: Read 2 Peter 1:5–11.

NO. 1 CHRISTY MATHEWSON Known as "The Christian Gentleman," Mathewson had to overcome his mom's strong desire for him to become a pastor. Instead, he won 372 games for the New York Giants (and one for the Cincinnati Reds) from 1900 through 1916 and was inducted into the Baseball Hall of Fame as a member of its first class in 1936. He wrote children's books after his career ended.

2. PLUGGERS, FOOZLES, AND SKYSCRAPERS

"It is God's will that you should be sanctified:
that you should avoid sexual immorality."

1 THESSALONIANS 4:3

Baseball used to be the most popular sport in the United States—far surpassing even pro football.

And in the game's heyday, some of the best writing in journalism came from baseball writers. The scribes invented all kinds of colorful new ways to describe the action on the field. After all, if you have to describe more than 150 games, you must be creative.

FAST FACT:

An English-born cricket writer, Henry Chadwick, first used the phrase "national pastime" about baseball.

For example, fans were once called *pluggers*, a stupid play on the field was a *foozle*, and a fly ball was dubbed a *skyscraper*. The dugout was the *dog kennel*, and a curveball was a *mackerel*.

Those words have gone the way of the doubleheader, day World Series games, and ERAs under 3. They no longer are a part of the vocabulary of baseball fans.

If we aren't careful, we as Christians might lose some of the most important words in our lexicon as well. Words like *purity*, *sanctification*, and *holiness*. These words are threatened with extinction because of the inconvenience they cause us.

It's not easy to be holy in a world that pushes the envelope of permissiveness at every turn. It's tough to be set apart (sanctified) when fewer and fewer of our friends care about that distinction. It's hard to remain sexually pure when there's such a lack of discretion in sexual matters in the community at large.

It doesn't matter if we don't have *pluggers*, *foozles*, and *skyscrapers* in baseball anymore. But we can't afford to lose words like *purity*, *sanctification*, and *holiness*. We need to keep these words on our lips and in our lives. They are words from God himself. And He never changes what He has in mind for us.

—DAVE BRANON

FOLLOW THROUGH

Think through the next week of your life. Are there some places you plan to go where purity, sanctification, or holiness will be compromised? How can a change of plans keep your heart closer to where it should be?

From the Playbook: Read 1 Thessalonians 4:1–12.

NO. 2 MIKE SCHMIDT The most prolific home run producing third baseman ever, Schmidt was introduced to Jesus Christ by missionary statesman Dr. Wendell Kempton in 1978. Schmidt hit 548 career home runs and was inducted into the Baseball Hall of Fame in 1995.

3. THE ACCIDENTAL PITCHER

*"Dear children, let us not love with words or tongue
but with actions and in truth."*

1 JOHN 3:18

One of the greatest closers of all time never even planned to be a pitcher.

Young Mariano Rivera was the shortstop for the Chorrera team in Panama, and that ball club already had a great pitcher. "But during one of our most important games," as Rivera explains it, "he was getting killed. I wanted to win so bad! So I pitched . . . and we won."

The next thing Rivera knew, a New York Yankees' scout was at his doorstep—inviting him to a tryout. In 1990, Rivera signed a contract with New York and left behind his father's sardine fishing boats and the family's 12x24-foot house.

The journey from Puerto Caimito, Panama, to Yankee Stadium wasn't much smoother than the gravel ball fields he played stickball on as a youth. In 1992 there was elbow surgery that raised doubts about his future, and in 1994 his wife became very ill.

"I have a huge family back home, but here I have nobody," Mariano said of that difficult episode. "I wasn't a Christian then. But every time I was going through a hard time, somebody was there to help. It's not too often when you have a minor league coach

FAST FACT:
The all-time leader in major league saves, Trevor Hoffman, started 2009 with 524. Lee Smith had 448. Rivera began 2009 with 482.

who will tell you he will take care of your son while you stay with your wife at the hospital. My pitching coach did that.

"And one lady from Panama—I never knew her before—offered to stay with my wife while I was playing. Even though I had nobody here, I was never alone. That led me to accept Jesus as my Savior. I knew it wasn't a coincidence. It was the Lord putting someone there for me."

Rivera makes frequent trips back to Panama to share the joy of his faith with kids playing stickball on the gravel fields down by the fishing docks.

What is keeping us from being "there to help" others, showing them love in word and deed and thus pointing them to Jesus?

—GWEN DIAZ

FOLLOW THROUGH

Think of a person who needs someone to love them to Jesus as happened with Mariano. What can you do for that person this week?

From the Playbook: Read 1 John 3:11–24.

NO 3 MARIANO RIVERA Considered by many the best closer ever, Rivera enjoys sharing his knowledge of baseball and his love for Jesus with others. "I've been blessed by the Lord to be able to share with kids." He was the MVP of the 1999 World Series.

4. TOO GOOD TO BE TRUE?

Strike Zone:
Contemplating God's great gift

"Thanks be to God for his indescribable gift!"
2 CORINTHIANS 9:15

In 1985, the New York Mets discovered a British orphan with a gifted arm living in Florida. Despite the fact that Sidd Finch had never played baseball, the Mets offered him a spot in the team's spring training camp—all based on the fact that Finch could deliver a 168-mph fastball.

Too good to be true? Well, actually, yes it was.

Finch was the creation of *Sports Illustrated* writer George Plimpton, who concocted the story for an April Fool's Day edition of the magazine. The story, which included a photo of the newly discovered phenomenon, made believers out of many baseball fans until Plimpton came clean two weeks later.

There's another story that seems too good to be true—but isn't. God provided us with the ultimate gift in giving us His Son Jesus, who died so that we may live. And each day, the Lord continues to bestow gifts and blessings on us that help us to serve Him better.

FAST FACT:
The Sidd Finch story elicited more than 2,000 letters to the editor at SI.

In 2 Corinthians 9, we are reminded of the many ways God demonstrates His love toward us, making us "rich in every way" (vs. 11) and that we are expected to give back to the Lord based on the way He has given to us.

And best of all, God will never come back in a few weeks and tell us that what He promised us was just a joke, a figment of our imagination.

So, considering everything you have received from the Lord, why not take a minute to thank Him for His wonderful gifts and see if there's a way you can use those gifts to live for Him.

—JEFF ARNOLD

FOLLOW THROUGH

What gift has God given you that makes you who you are? Take a few minutes today and consider how you're using that gift and if there is a way you could use it on a daily basis to live better for Jesus.

From the Playbook: Read 2 Corinthians 9.

NO. 4 PAUL MOLITOR Molitor was a hit machine. He had 190 or more hits in a season seven times and ended with 3,319 hits—ninth best ever. His name was enshrined at Cooperstown in 2004. During his career, he said, "I try to emulate Christ in everything I do."

5. FRIENDLY MOTIVATION

"Stimulate one another to love and good deeds."
HEBREWS 10:24 (NAS)

When veteran big league hurlers John Smoltz (Atlanta Braves) and Tom Glavine (then New York Mets) hooked up against each other on May 25, 2007, a longtime friendship turned into a challenge of historic proportions.

Smoltz and Glavine were teammates on the Atlanta Braves' pitching staff from 1988 through 2002. They were part of one of the best starting rotations in baseball history. Glavine signed a free-agent deal to pitch for the rival New York Mets beginning in 2003.

FAST FACT:

John Smoltz was the first major league pitcher to reach 200 wins and 150 saves.

But in May 2007, the two friends opposed each other in a game that would make baseball history. Smoltz would win the 200th game of his Hall of Fame career against his friend and former teammate.

He told the *New York Times*, "I can tell you who my 200th victory is and 15 years from now, I'll still remember it."

Friends have a way of challenging us. They can stimulate us to greater achievements than we might accomplish on our own.

On the journey of faith, we need others to stimulate us, encourage us, and challenge us toward a more active and engaging Christian life.

That's why the writer of Hebrews challenged first-century Christians "to stimulate" each other toward a life focused on God's mission for us on earth. North American-based believers may not experience persecution as many early Christians did, yet we need the encouragement and motivation of fellow believers to press on faithfully through the curves life throws our way.

Who are you stimulating on their journey of faith? Is there someone in your life you can encourage to greater actions of love and deeds that honor God?

—Rob Bentz

FOLLOW THROUGH

Ask God in prayer to reveal someone in your life who you can stimulate on toward love and good deeds in their walk with Jesus.

From the Playbook: Meditate on Hebrews 10:24–25.

NO. 5 JOHN SMOLTZ   Not many pitchers become a great starter and a great reliever. When arm problems forced him to the bullpen late in his career, he racked up 100 saves in two seasons. The 1996 Cy Young Award winner, Smoltz has 15 postseason victories—the most all-time. "In the end," he says, "all you have is Christ, and all you have as a man is your word. Those are the things I stand on."

6. SCHILLING'S FAITH

"Since we have been justified through faith, we have peace with God through our Lord Jesus Christ."

ROMANS 5:1

Curt Schilling has been one of baseball's true aces for more than a decade. He's won the biggest of games. He's won the most prestigious of trophies. The guy has had a stellar big league career.

Why? He worked hard. Schilling studied hitters. He was always prepared. No hitter stepped into the box against the future Hall of Fame righthander without having been scrutinized by Schilling as he studied notes and reports on that batter's tendencies. The guy worked at his craft to be the best.

Yet there is one more thing Schilling credits for his success. Faith. Not faith in his abilities (although he certainly has a measure of that also). Not faith in his efforts.

Schilling has faith in Jesus Christ. "My faith is my cornerstone and my foundation," he says. "You're counted on to be good, and when it doesn't work out you deal with it. It was a personal struggle, but faith has always been a good thing to me. It got me through the 2004 season [the year Boston won their first World Series in 86 years], and it's getting me through today," Schilling told *American Way* magazine.

FAST FACT:
Curt Schilling was a three-time 20-game winner during his major league career.

In his letter to the Romans, Paul outlines the importance of faith in Jesus Christ. Faith in Jesus and His work on the cross is what justifies the believer. Faith in Jesus gives peace. Faith in Jesus opens the door for God's grace and mercy to flow in and through you.

Do you have faith in Jesus?

— ROB BENTZ

FOLLOW THROUGH

If you desire to place your faith in Jesus, talk to God in the words of the following prayer: "God, I confess that I am a sinner in need of your forgiveness. I repent of my sin, and place my faith in Jesus Christ, who lived a holy life and gave that life as a payment for my sin. Thank you for taking control of my life. Amen."

From the Playbook: Read Romans 5:1–11.

NO. 6 CURT SCHILLING With 216 wins and 3,116 strikeouts, Schilling is assured a spot in the Hall of Fame. But his most memorable moment came in the 2004 playoffs when he defied a serious foot injury to will the Boston Red Sox to a win—bloody sock and all. "I have never in my life been touched by God like I was tonight," he said. "Tonight was God's work, no question."

7. DON'T GIVE UP

"Jesus said, 'Feed my sheep.'"
JOHN 21:17

On the last day of spring training in 1979, Steve Kemp of the Detroit Tigers was hit in the head with a pitched ball. The injury was serious enough that he had to be taken to the hospital.

But on the very next afternoon—Opening Day of the regular season—he stepped up to the plate with confidence against the Texas Rangers. Taking fastballs from future Hall of Fame pitcher Ferguson Jenkins, Kemp smacked a single. The next time at bat he hit a home run.

During a postgame interview he said, "After I was hit, I just told myself, 'I can't let it bother me.' If you let it bother you, you're not going to be any good to yourself or your team."

FAST FACT:

The Tigers lost that Opening Day game in 1979 to the Rangers 7-2.

The apostle Peter responded to a bitter experience in much the same way. He had been hit hard by a "pitch" from the enemy. He had promised earlier that he would follow Christ, even if it meant death (Matthew 26:33–35). But just a little while later, while facing unexpected pressure, he denied his Lord (vv. 69–75).

That devastating blow could have caused him to quit. But Peter didn't give up—because Jesus didn't give up on him. After the Lord encouraged him (John 21:15–19), Peter boldly proclaimed the gospel, and many people trusted in Christ.

26

Have you been hit by failure? Don't give up. The Lord wants to restore you and make you useful again.

—Mart De Haan

FOLLOW THROUGH

What "bean ball" has knocked you down? Are you willing to get up, dust yourself off, and go back up to the plate again in life—with God's help?

From the Playbook: Read Matthew 26:69–75.

NO. 7 JACKIE ROBINSON It's been said that Branch Rickey said "The Life of Christ" was the reason he chose to break baseball's color barrier. And he chose a man of quiet Christian conviction to do the hard part. Robinson's teammate with the Brooklyn Dodgers Carl Erskine said Robinson was "a man devoted to his God and to the ideals set forth in the Bible." Robinson hit .311 in his 10-year career and was inducted into the Hall of Fame in 1962.

8. OPENING DAY

*"If anyone is in Christ, he is a new creation;
the old has gone, the new has come!"*

2 CORINTHIANS 5:17

Nobody liked Opening Day quite as much as Walter Johnson. The "Big Train" hurled nine shutouts in 14 Opening Day starts. One was a 15-inning, 1-0 classic against the Philadelphia Athletics. Even perennial losers like Johnson's Washington Senators could claim to be in first place after he pitched the opener.

But the cliché "the season is a marathon" is still true! The season isn't won or lost in a game. The Senators of the early twentieth century usually tumbled to the American League basement by June.

FAST FACT:
The Cincinnati Reds, baseball's oldest professional team, is the only major league club that always opens the season at home.

We who have a personal relationship with Jesus sometimes compare our salvation to a new start. And that's true. "If anyone is in Christ, he is a new creation; the old has gone, the new has come!" (2 Corinthians 5:17). The forgiveness God gives us through the redeeming death of His Son Jesus represents a brand-new beginning for every believer.

Eventually, though, the Christian life plods on into the dog days of August. The exhilaration we felt when we first received Christ erodes as friends, family, and church let us down—and often, we let God down! What then?

God's prophetic words to the church in Ephesus have application for us in the 21st century. Despite the Ephesians' great start, He still had something against them. "You have forsaken your first love," He said (Revelation 2:4). A church that had done so much good in its community was doing so out of obligation and not out of the zeal the people first enjoyed.

Are you plodding through the dog days of August in your walk with Jesus? Ask God to give you a renewed zeal for Him and His Word. Experience the joy of our personal Opening Day all over again.

—TIM GUSTAFSON

FOLLOW THROUGH

How does my walk with Christ compare to the day I first received Him? What can I do to recapture that "first love"? Can I point to a time when I made my relationship with Jesus a personal thing?

From the Playbook: Read Revelation 2:1–7.

NO. 8 DUKE SNIDER Snider was another of Jackie Robinson's teammates, debuting for the Dodgers just two days after Robinson did in 1947. Snider retired in 1964 with 407 home runs and a .295 average. The Duke, inducted into the Hall in 1980, says, "Christianity works—with Jesus living in you and through you."

9. FUTURE SIGHT

*"It is not for you to know the times or dates the
Father has set by his own authority."*

ACTS 1:7

When it comes to baseball trades, hindsight is always 20/20. What looks like a win-win deal on paper can become lopsided in a hurry! If there ever was a second chance given to general managers in the big leagues, the following trades would never have happened:

- 1964: The Chicago Cubs sent OF Lou Brock to the St. Louis Cardinals for OF Ernie Broglio. Brock is in the Hall of Fame. Broglio, not so much.
- 1987: The Detroit Tigers sent P John Smoltz to the Atlanta Braves for P Doyle Alexander. Smoltz gave the Braves more than 20 years of excellence; Alexander retired in 1989.
- 1990: The Boston Red Sox sent 1B Jeff Bagwell to the Houston Astros for RP Larry Andersen. Bagwell hit 449 home runs for the Astros; Andersen won exactly zero games for Boston.

FAST FACT:

John Smoltz won the 1996 Cy Young Award for the Atlanta Braves.

The Cubs, Tigers, and Red Sox obviously couldn't see into the future. If they could have, they would not have traded future baseball Hall of Famers. But major league general managers can't see into the future. And neither can we.

We don't know what tomorrow will bring. We can't tell if next week will bring us blessing or suffering.

Only God can see into the future. The Trinitarian God we serve is all knowing. The theological term for this is *omniscience*. It means that "God knows all things in the past, in the present, and in the future."

In Acts 1:7, following Jesus' death, burial, and resurrection Jesus tells His apostles that the time and dates of the coming kingdom are *"not for you to know."* Only God knows.

The journey of faith is just that—faith. We walk through life each day not knowing the future, yet trusting that God is in control and knows what He's doing. Only our omniscient God has future sight.

—ROB BENTZ

FOLLOW THROUGH

Research the following verses that tell us more about God's omniscience: Matthew 10:30; Psalm 147:4; and Isaiah 40:26.

From the Playbook: Read Acts 1:1–11.

NO. 9 LOU BROCK The World Series belonged to Lou Brock. In his three fall classics, he hit .391. The second greatest base-stealer ever, Brock stole 118 bases in 1974. But Brock knows true greatness: "Jesus Christ is a name greater than any other name. It's the only name that will get you into heaven." Brock got into the National Baseball Hall of Fame in 1985.

10. THE 400-HOMER SEASON

*"Because you are my help, I sing in the
shadow of your wings."*

PSALM 63:7

Baseball season brings out the sports geek in me. For instance, I like making absurd projections based on early-season performances. On Opening Day in 2005, Dmitri Young slugged three home runs for the Detroit Tigers. At that pace, I figured, he would hit 486 dingers. He didn't, of course. He wound up with 21.

Even month-long records are misleading. Sammy Sosa once clubbed 20 homers in a month, yet he never approached 120 for a year. The arduous season always imposes its will on gaudy short-term statistics. The cliché is true—a baseball season is a marathon, not a sprint. A player must persevere through both up and down times over the long haul.

FAST FACT:
The record for home runs in April is 14, jointly held by Alex Rodriguez (2007) and Albert Pujols (2006).

King David didn't know baseball, but he knew persistence. He gained fame early in life by slaying a giant and leading Israel to stunning military victories. But David's psalms often tell of "slumps" and dry spells. When he penned Psalm 63, he wrote from a literal desert, which prompted this powerful imagery about desiring God: "My soul thirsts for you, my body longs for you, in a dry and weary land where there is no water" (v. 1).

So what did David do in the dry times? He started by recalling the Lord's goodness: "I have seen you in the sanctuary and beheld your power and your glory. Because your love is better than life" (vv. 2–3). This review of God's strength and goodness enabled David to find hope. "I will praise you as long as I live," he exclaimed. "My soul will be satisfied" (vv. 4–5). In the end, David was seen as a man "after [God's] own heart" (1 Samuel 13:14; Acts 13:22).

God isn't looking for flashy statistics. He's looking for consistent obedience to Him, even in the tough times. That's the kind of "player" He can make into a champion!

—Tim Gustafson

FOLLOW THROUGH

Why is it wrong for a believer in Jesus to trust in his own abilities? What do I do when times get tough? Have I ever written down what God has done for me?

From the Playbook: Read Psalm 63.

NO. 10 BUCK LEONARD In 1948, Buck Leonard hit .395. Even though this was a year after Jackie Robinson broke baseball's color barrier, by then Leonard was 41 years old, and he was playing in one of the last years of the Negro Leagues for the Homestead (PA) Grays. Leonard retired with a .342 lifetime average. When he was inducted into the Hall of Fame in 1972 with his old friend Josh Gibson, Leonard told the crowd, "It's nice to receive praise and honor of men, but the greatest praise and honor comes from our Lord and Savior, Jesus Christ."

11. DON'T EVEN THINK ABOUT GIVING UP

Strike Zone:
Enduring tough times

"You need to persevere so that when you have done the will of God, you will receive what he has promised."

HEBREWS 10:36

After the first twenty-one games of the 1988 baseball season, the Baltimore Orioles had found a way to lose 21 games. That's right—all of them. Manager Cal Ripken, Sr. was fired after six games, and with the majority of the season yet to be played, new manager Frank Robinson had no other choice but to tell his team to just keep on playing.

The Orioles, who had lost 95 games the previous year, ended up with a record of 54-107. Not exactly championship-level baseball.

Sometimes in our lives we go through slumps when things don't seem to go our way, making it difficult to even keep moving forward. Sometimes we feel like just throwing our arms in the air and giving up.

Don't.

In Hebrews 10, we learn that many times God allows us to go through tough times only to reward us in the end. "You need to persevere so that when you have done the will of God, you will receive what he has promised" (v. 36). As hard as it is sometimes, we need to keep working through the obstacles that life puts in front of us.

FAST FACT:

Former major league baseball play-by-play announcer (and then-President) Ronald Reagan called Frank Robinson during the winless streak to offer his support.

God wants us to continue to give Him our all, which means we have to ignore the temptation to get angry or give up.

Often, God will teach us something about His character as we depend on Him to get us through the difficult days. God has promised us that if we live according to His will, He will deliver on His promise of eternal rewards (Hebrews 9:15).

—JEFF ARNOLD

FOLLOW THROUGH

Are you trying to fight your way out of one of life's losing streaks? Ask God for patience and wisdom as you try to work through it, and you'll find that He is faithful.

From the Playbook: Read Hebrews 10.

NO. 11 ALBERT PUJOLS Arguably the greatest player in the twenty-first century, Pujols burst on the scene in 2001 with 37 home runs, 194 hits, 130 RBI, and a .329 batting average. And the stats just kept piling up. In 2005, he was the National League MVP at the age of 25. Rookie of the Year in 2001. Major League Player of the Year in 2003. National League Championship Series in 2004. And he was just getting started. Kind of like his faith. In 2007, he said, "I'm still a baby in Christ. I keep learning and just follow my Leader—follow the things the Lord wants me to do."

12. SHE THROWS LIKE A GIRL

Strike Zone:
Challenging today's society

"Who knows but that you have come to royal position for such a time as this?"

ESTHER 4:14

On May 14, 2005, an 11-year-old girl named Katie Brownell threw like a girl . . . and made history. The quiet, 5-foot-8 preteen from Oakfield, New York, became the first girl in Little League baseball history to pitch a perfect game. In the six-inning game, Katie struck out all 18 batters she faced—and they all happened to be boys. In fact, not one batter got even close to getting on base—none even got as far as a three-ball count. Katie was the only girl on the Dodger team, and she's the only girl to throw a perfect game. Katie broke the cultural norms for a girl and unexpectedly turned lots of heads.

FAST FACT:
In 1974, 30,000 girls registered to play Little League. Today, about 400,000 girls play Little League baseball and softball.

Several thousand years ago, a young Jewish girl named Esther also discovered what it feels like to break cultural norms. In a day when girls had little to no freedom or authority, Esther stepped outside her expected role to risk her life to help God's people, the Jews. Risking her security and her life, Esther said, "I will go to the king, even though it is against the law. And if I perish, I perish" (Esther 4:16).

What about you? Would you consider being used by God to challenge cultural norms in an increasingly godless world? If you trust Him and do not fear, He can use you to do things that others might be afraid to even consider. Look for God-given opportunities to change society. Then seize the day!

—MOLLY RAMSEYER

FOLLOW THROUGH

What cultural norms have you subscribed to without thinking? Ask God today to call to mind a way that you can stand out for Him by challenging some negative aspect of culture.

From the Playbook: Read the book of Esther—it promises to captivate your attention!

NO. 12 TODD HELTON From 1998 through 2007, Helton hit over .300 every season—including a remarkable .372 in 2000 with 42 home runs and 147 RBI. Helton has also won the Gold Glove Award several times for his defensive work at first base. Two years after his signature season, Helton and his wife welcomed their daughter Tierney into the world. He said of her birth, "I wanted my daughter to grow up and to see dad doing the right things. You want your child to grow up and walk with Christ and know Him at an early age."

13. ARKY AND PIE

"[Barnabas] was a good man, full of the Holy Spirit and faith, and a great number of people were brought to the Lord."

ACTS 11:24

Arky Vaughan is a name that's hard to forget. But unless you're a big fan of baseball history, it's likely that you've never heard of him.

Arky hit .318 over 14 major-league seasons and was posthumously inducted into the Baseball Hall of Fame in 1985. Born in 1912, Vaughan was an extraordinary hitter who taught himself to be an excellent shortstop. So why isn't Arky celebrated the same as other legends of the game—the Babe Ruths, Ty Cobbs, Pie Traynors?

FAST FACT:
Arky's .385 batting average in 1935 was the best by a shortstop in the twentieth century.

Well, for a good part of his career, Arky played with Pie Traynor! Considered one of the greatest third basemen of all time, Traynor and his brilliance simply outshone Arky Vaughan's star qualities. Playing on the same team as Traynor made Mr. Vaughan and his stats appear somewhat humble.

In the book of Acts we read about two men who were catalysts in spreading the gospel of Jesus and establishing the early church. Their names were Paul and Barnabas.

Today, we don't hesitate to celebrate the life and teachings of Paul, for he was led by the Holy Spirit to write most of the books of the New Testament. During the time Paul and Barnabas spent together, Paul was also recognized as the "chief speaker" of the two (14:12).

But Barnabas? Well, he is remembered for his encouraging ways and steady faith, but Paul stands out in the pages of Scripture and in our thinking.

Has God called you to be a Barnabas—to minister effectively for Him behind others who are more visible and acclaimed? Humbly and eagerly accept that call, for your goal is to serve Jesus selflessly—seeking God's "well done," not the praise of people (Philippians 2:3).

—Tom Felten

FOLLOW THROUGH

Write the names "Paul" and "Barnabas" at the top of a piece of paper. Underneath each name, write the gifts and abilities each possessed. Then pray and thank God for the gifts and abilities that He has given you—to be used for His glory!

From the Playbook: Read Acts 11:19–30.

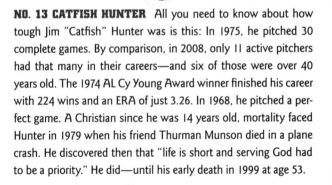

NO. 13 CATFISH HUNTER All you need to know about how tough Jim "Catfish" Hunter was is this: In 1975, he pitched 30 complete games. By comparison, in 2008, only 11 active pitchers had that many in their careers—and six of those were over 40 years old. The 1974 AL Cy Young Award winner finished his career with 224 wins and an ERA of just 3.26. In 1968, he pitched a perfect game. A Christian since he was 14 years old, mortality faced Hunter in 1979 when his friend Thurman Munson died in a plane crash. He discovered then that "life is short and serving God had to be a priority." He did—until his early death in 1999 at age 53.

14. ONE MAN'S FUTURE

*"I will instruct you and teach you in the way you should go;
I will counsel you and watch over you."*

PSALM 32:8

Early in his baseball career, All-Star first baseman Lance Berkman was already thinking beyond his playing days.

"I want to start a church," said Berkman of his future plans, adding that his dream fellowship would be located in Houston. "I've got some ideas about the kind of church it would be. There is so much division in church today. I think we've gotten away from the true gospel, which is Jesus Christ, Him crucified, and His love that He showed to the masses, and the way He dealt with people.

FAST FACT:

In 2002, Lance Berkman led the National League in runs batted in with 128.

"I think what He calls us to do is to love as many people into the kingdom as we can. The kind of church I want to have is straight-from-the-Bible teaching, line-by-line, verse-by-verse, and at the same time a body that is truly active in the community to show the love of Christ."

When most athletes talk about goals, they speak of certain statistical plateaus, or a championship, or the Hall of Fame. Lance Berkman may attain all of those, but only as part of a greater purpose, a purpose he doesn't completely understand yet but one in which he is confident of God's leading.

"I can totally see the hand of God working in my life, dictating a path here or there. It is mind-boggling when I stop and think about how He has controlled the path and blessed me."

Major league slugger Lance Berkman listened for God's leading, and he allowed it to give him a direction for the future. He seems to know where he's going. He has a plan to follow God in the years ahead.

Do you?

—Victor Lee

FOLLOW THROUGH

Can you say with any certainty what God has planned for you in the next months or years? How has God led you in the past? How are you seeking His guidance today?

From the Playbook: Read Psalm 32:8–11.

NO. 14 LANCE BERKMAN We came very close to never hearing of Lance Berkman. Undrafted after high school, he had just one college coach who was interested in him. Berkman took Rice University's offer, and by the time he was a junior he was the best player in college and a first-round draft pick of Houston. Three hundred home runs and a thousand RBI later, Berkman understands his responsibility as a Christian: "The Lord has blessed me with success on the field, and He expects me to be a witness for Him and share what He's done for my life."

15. THE IAMT PRINCIPLE

"If your brother sins against you, go and show him his fault, just between the two of you."

MATTHEW 18:15

Ernie Lombardi could hit, but he sure couldn't run! Lombardi is the only catcher to win two batting titles, but his lack of speed was also legendary. In fact, infielders could play him so deep that Lombardi once confessed that Dodgers' shortstop Pee Wee Reese "was in the league 3 years before I realized he wasn't an outfielder."

FAST FACT:
Lombardi hit over .300 in 10 of his 17 major league seasons. His lifetime batting average was .306.

Lombardi won his first batting title with Cincinnati in 1938, hitting .342 and winning NL MVP honors. However, after struggling at the plate in 1941, Lombardi was traded by Reds general manager Warren Giles to the Boston Braves, only to have the slow-footed but hard-hitting catcher win the second of his batting titles with a .330 average in 1942.

The two had argued publicly, mainly over salary issues, with Lombardi calling Giles "the old goat." Decades later, the still bitter Giles, himself an influential member of the Hall of Fame, successfully lobbied against Lombardi's election to Cooperstown. Only after both men passed away did the Veteran's Committee name Ernie to the Hall in 1986.

What a sad commentary that they would both go to the grave holding tightly to their grudge. Neither was willing to do the right thing—which is to go to the other to attempt to restore their relationship.

In Matthew 18, Jesus talked to His disciples about how to handle those times when believers experience disagreements. The process of healing a broken relationship doesn't begin by waiting for the other person to come to you. It begins with the "*It's Always My Turn*" principle. Although not every situation may get resolved, you are responsible to start the process that can lead to forgiveness and restoration. Don't be slow afoot like Ernie Lombardi. Remember IAMT, and make the first move.

—BRIAN HETTINGA

FOLLOW THROUGH

Do you really want people to remember you for your ability to hold a grudge? Apply the IAMT principle to a disagreement you have with someone this week.

From the Playbook: Read the four-step process of confrontation, repentance, forgiveness, and restoration Jesus outlined in Matthew 18:15–20.

NO. 15 GARY CARTER He's been retired from baseball for a long time, but he's still The Kid. Gregarious and outspoken, Carter piled up 324 home runs and 11 All-Star Game selections during his career. But the Hall of Fame didn't call his name until 11 years after he hung up his mask. He learned that "when you don't have control of something, you just take it out of your hands altogether and put it in God's hands."

16. WHO BELIEVES IN YOU?

"You guide me with your counsel."

PSALM 73:24

When I was a senior in high school, I enjoyed doing the recruiting trip thing in North Texas. I was visiting a small college that had a good reputation in baseball as well as academics. I was invited to the afternoon practice by the baseball coach. I had a great workout, and the coach pulled me into the office to tell me that he was going to grant me a scholarship to come and play baseball for him. Both my mother and I were pretty excited about his offer.

FAST FACT:

Jeremy attended Northwest Christian High School near Spokane, Washington. He was drafted after his senior year by Kansas City.

Then he said something else to me before I left his office. "Jeremy, I think you are a great baseball player, and you can play for a lot of bigger schools. You obviously can play for me, but I don't think you are good enough to play professional baseball." I got up and shook his hand and said my goodbyes.

On the flight back to Washington, my mother was really excited about the scholarship until I broke the news to her. "Mom, I can't play for that man." When she asked why, I told her that I could never play for a man who could look me in the eye and tell me that I am not good enough.

If God gives you a talent and a dream, you need to put yourself in a position to achieve that dream. You have to surround yourself with people who believe in you and who are willing to encourage you to achieve your dreams. How you choose your friends and whom you allow into your circle of trust will have a huge effect on whether your dreams will become a reality. God has a will for you, but it's up to you to achieve it.

—JEREMY AFFELDT

FOLLOW THROUGH

What talent, skill, or interest has God given you that you feel He wants you to use greatly? Who do you know who can encourage you toward the goal of using what God has given you?

From the Playbook: Read Proverbs 15:22–23.

NO. 16 ANDRE DAWSON His numbers are Hall of Fame-like. His problem? Injuries. If he had played healthy, perhaps his numbers would have crossed all of the HOF thresholds. Dawson credited his grandmother with leading him to faith in Jesus Christ, and he lived out that faith throughout his career, which ended after 21 seasons with 2,774 hits, 438 home runs, and 1,591 RBI.

17. FASTBALL FEARS

"The one who is in you is greater than the one who is in the world."

1 JOHN 4:4

It is possible to concentrate so intently on the great power of our spiritual enemy Satan that we set ourselves up for defeat.

We are sometimes like the baseball players who had to face Sandy Koufax, the Hall of Fame pitcher for the Los Angeles Dodgers in the 1960s. According to Jim Kaat, another great pitcher, "Koufax was the only major-league pitcher whose fastball could be heard to hum. Opposing batters, instead of being noisily active in their dugout, would sit silently and listen for that fastball to hum. They would then take their turn at the plate already intimidated."

FAST FACT:

Sandy Koufax threw four no-hitters in his major league pitching career.

Satan is an intimidating adversary. He is the master of deceit, the motivator of murder, and the instigator of false teaching. But fascination with his tricks and fear of his tactics must not become central in our minds. Rather, we must focus on who we are—God's children. We have already overcome the evil one through faith in Christ (1 John 4:4), and we can overcome him now through the power of the indwelling Holy Spirit.

There are victories to be won in the Christian life, but not if we concentrate on Satan's frightening roar (1 Peter 5:8). It does us no good to sit and think about his power. Instead, we need to ask the Lord to help us have the discernment to recognize what Satan is doing—then depend on God's strength. He who is in us is greater than he who is in the world. That's a thought worth dwelling on.

—DAVE BRANON

FOLLOW THROUGH

What do you think some of Satan's favorite tricks are as he tries to influence people to do wrong things? How are you making sure his tricks don't dupe you?

From the Playbook: Read 1 John 4:1–6.

NO. 17 JIM KAAT During his days as a major league pitcher, Kaat did more than win 283 games and put his name in contention for consideration by Hall of Fame voters. He took with him his faith from his historically devout community of Zeeland, Michigan, and helped establish Baseball Chapel. He was a team leader for chapels in the early days of that outreach in baseball. Kaat pitched in the majors from 1959 through 1983.

18. THE JOB AT HAND

*"Whatever you do, work at it with all your heart,
as working for the Lord, not for men."*

COLOSSIANS 3:23

It's easy to get your mind off what you are doing and start worrying about something that might be coming up later. This is especially true for a major league pitcher.

When you see a great hitter standing in the on-deck circle, for example, you have to concentrate even more on the guy you are facing at the time. The reason for this is simple: You don't want to allow the batter to get on base so the great hitter comes up with a runner on base. If you keep the first batter off the bases, then if you do make a mistake on the great hitter and he smacks one out of the park, it's only a solo shot and not a two-run home run. So, focusing on the job at hand may help you out later.

FAST FACT:

Brandon and his wife Alicia help underprivileged youth through their K-Foundation. Read about it at www. brandonwebb.org.

What's true of pitching is true of life. If you make good decisions every day along the way, good things have a better chance of happening later.

What has God given you to do right now? What good decisions and actions does He want from you today? How can you honor Him with a good decision?

Don't worry so much about what might be coming later. God will help you with that when the time comes. Focus instead on the job at hand.

—BRANDON WEBB

FOLLOW THROUGH

We should not just focus on our own problems. We should look for ways to help others as much as God allows us to. Look for opportunities to focus on the life of others and assist them. It might even help you regain some personal focus.

From the Playbook: Read all 25 verses of Colossians 3 and see other areas that God wants us to focus on.

NO. 18 TOMMY JOHN No, he is not a doctor. But his name is associated with a medical procedure—Tommy John surgery. When Dr. Frank Jobe successfully fixed John's arm in 1974 by moving a tendon from another part of his body to his pitching arm, the term was born. John won 288 games in his 26-year career—including three 20-plus-win seasons after Dr. Jobe repaired his arm. A short movie, *The Tommy John Story*, was filmed in 1979 to tell about John's recovery and his faith.

19. I WAS THERE

"The life appeared; we have seen it and testify to it."
1 JOHN 1:2

As a longtime baseball fan, I've been at some pretty signifi-cant major league ballgames. I've been in attendance at a record-setting home run derby (Chicago White Sox-Detroit Tigers), a game in which a veteran superstar reached a major career milestone (Johnny Bench), and even the last game ever played at an historic stadium (Tiger Stadium). I've seen a lot of bizarre, impressive, and unfor-gettable moments. I can literally tell my base-ball buddies, "I was there!"

FAST FACT:

On May 29, 1995, the Sox and Tigers combined for 12 homers! And Rob Bentz was there.

The same can be said of the apostle John. But what He witnessed up close and personal was not just a game. He saw the Savior. John spent one-on-one time with Jesus. He saw Him do the miraculous and the mundane. He wit-nessed the wonders of our Lord. He was literally there. That's why he begins the first of his letters telling his friends in the faith, in effect, "I was there!"

John starts off his first letter by establishing the credibility of what he has to say in the writing that follows. In the first verse of the first chapter of his first letter, John emphasizes three "there" moments. John tells us that he and the other apostles have "seen with our eyes," have "looked at," and "our hands have touched" Jesus. Yes, John was actually there.

This is critical, because John then follows these statements with details of the incarnation of Jesus—that Christ did indeed rise from the dead!

You and I did not see or hear Jesus after His resurrection the way John did. We were not there. But John was there! We can trust his testimony because he saw and heard and touched the risen Christ.

"I was there," John proclaims. And he verifies it: Jesus has risen!

—ROB BENTZ

FOLLOW THROUGH

Read about and meditate on the significance of what John is writing in today's text. Jesus defeated death, rose from the grave, and spent time on earth with John and the other apostles. Spend a few moments praising God for His victory.

From the Playbook: Read 1 John 1–4.

19 ANDY PETTITTE When Andy Pettitte messed up, he fessed up. Shortly after the Mitchell Report noted that the lefty had used Human Growth Hormone (HGH), Pettitte admitted what he had done, and he apologized. Christians aren't perfect, just forgiven, as the bumper sticker says. Pettitte didn't really need any help. His winning percentage is in the Top 50 of all time, and he has won more than 200 games. He also knows the value of keeping himself accountable. "I believe as a Christian man, you have to have partners to run with, guys to keep you accountable."

20. NUMBER 714

"Fix these words of mine in your hearts and minds."
DEUTERONOMY 11:18

It was the bottom of the ninth for a mythic career, and Babe Ruth should have already hung up his spikes. But the proud and prodigious Sultan of Swat had a little bit left.

On May 25, 1935, playing for the woeful Boston Braves against the Pittsburgh Pirates, the Bambino dragged his .150 average into the batter's box and became the first player to hit the ball over Forbes Field's right-field roof. It was his 714th and last home run. And his third that game! On May 30, Babe Ruth retired from baseball.

FAST FACT:
Babe Ruth had the most multi-home run games in major league history with 72.

My son and I can't get enough baseball history. But those great stories have come down to us through eyewitnesses—people who saw the events first-hand and passed on the news. If they hadn't cared, the stories would have died with them. And so I tell my son stories. Great stories are why the great game will thrive.

Before Moses made his last "plate appearance," he reminded Israel of some pretty impressive stories about God's greatness. He recounted the parting of the Red Sea and the drowning of the Egyptian army, the judgment of those who dared to challenge the Lord, and His miraculous provision of manna for 40 years.

Then Moses reminded parents to instruct their children, who had not seen these miracles first-hand. "Fix these words of mine in your hearts and minds," he said. "Teach them to your children" (Deuteronomy 11:18–19). They were even to write them on doorframes and gates. Moses sought to preserve a godly legacy by retelling stories.

God's greatness is not to be relegated to the archives and forgotten. It should be told and retold to everyone—especially the children.

—Tim Gustafson

FOLLOW THROUGH

Make a Top 5 list of the things God has done for you. Have you shared your stories with anyone? Is there someone younger than you whom you can mentor?

From the Playbook: Read Deuteronomy 11:1–7, 18–21.

NO. 20 OREL HERSHISER Hershiser picked a good time to peak. In 1988, from August through October, he put together among the best three months of any pitcher ever: 59 consecutive shutout innings, a 3-0 postseason record with an ERA of just over 1, and a nifty rendition of "The Doxology" on *The Tonight Show Starring Johnny Carson*. Then he wrote a book called *Out of the Blue* and went on to win 204 games.

21. SOMETIMES YOU LOSE

"Consider it pure joy, my brothers, whenever you face trials of many kinds."

JAMES 1:2

In the spring of 1971, I was a member of our high school baseball team. We finished the regular season without losing a game and were rated the No. 1 high school team in Northern California. We entered the postseason Tournament of Champions as the No. 1 seed.

FAST FACT:
Dr. Karl Payne has spent considerable time assisting the players of the Seattle Seahawks as their chaplain.

We began that season with one Christian on the team—a guy who was verbal enough about his faith to be labeled a "Jesus Freak." By the end of the season, eight players had made a public profession of faith in Jesus Christ as their Lord and Savior. We decided to get together before the first game of the tournament for our first official prayer meeting. One of the guys ended our prayer session by saying, "and thank you God that you are going to help us win this game." We all figured we just *had* to win this game because we had actually gotten together to pray, and we had asked God for His blessing.

Well, you can guess what happened that afternoon. We lost our first and only game of the season.

Until that point, we had not learned an important lesson: Trials are a normal and necessary part of Christian living. Trials that come from the hand of God are designed to equip and prepare us for future ministry. They make us stronger. Trials cannot be avoided, and anyone telling you they are optional in the life of a believer is mistaken. As young Christians, we thought God was there to help us avoid all trials. We learned that He is there to help us grow through them.

God's purpose when we face any trial from His hand is to give us endurance—to make our faith and character stronger. Trials are used to complete and mature us, so that we can be used as instruments in God's hand to serve Him in a variety of circumstances. Sometimes you lose—but God can turn even that into victory.

—KARL PAYNE

FOLLOW THROUGH

What do you think when you hear people, even preachers, suggest that the Christian life can be free of trials? Does Scripture support that thinking?

From the Playbook: Read James 1:2–18.

NO. 21 JOHN WETTELAND Before Mariano Rivera began shutting things down for New York's ninth innings, John Wetteland was there to do the job. He had 31 saves for the Yankees in 1995 and 43 in 1996. This was after he had 105 for Montreal and before he saved 150 games for Texas. Three hundred thirty saves, all told, before he retired to his Texas home, where he works with teenagers. "When God allows me to speak to kids, I can use that same intensity [from his pitching days] to talk about the Lord."

22. LET GOD TAKE CARE OF THE REST

*"For it is by grace you have been saved, through faith—
and this is not from yourselves, it is the gift of God."*

EPHESIANS 2:8

As a child I was diagnosed with ADD and extreme hyper-activity. That's a bad combination for someone living with strict schooling by nuns and parents who are just hoping their son can fall asleep at night.

FAST FACT:
Paul Byrd wrote a book called Free Byrd. *It was published during the 2008 baseball season.*

In sports, however, it was a much different story. I loved playing any sport, so I would practice and work really hard to succeed. Whatever sport I was playing at the moment was my passion. In baseball, I forced myself to concentrate on the mound, and I worked hard. Although I was small, I was able to go to college on a baseball scholarship and eventually turn pro after my junior year at LSU. Nonetheless, I was empty.

After four years of hearing people share the gospel with me, I collapsed. I had worked hard to be a good person, but my attempts and my walls of self-sufficiency caved in.

I thought working hard was the answer to Christianity. So off to work I went—performing for Jesus. More Bible study. More memorization. More "how to" books. More sharing. More scratching my head. Was I missing something?

I was exhausted, which was a good thing. Finally, I got it. I realized I needed to be redeemed, and I trusted Jesus as Savior. I realized there was nothing I could do—only what He could give me. Instead of trusting that He was big enough to change me and live through me, I had tried to attain my goal by human effort. As we learned from Simon (read Acts 8:1–25), we cannot receive God by giving money. And we can't receive Him by hard work (Ephesians 2:8–9).

Do you want Jesus as your Savior? Faith, not works, is what He wants. Then He'll take care of the rest.

—Paul Byrd

FOLLOW THROUGH

Does this "faith, not works" idea sound too good to be true? Examine the verses in Ephesians 2:8–9 and then act on them.

From the Playbook: Read Romans 3 and 4.

NO. 22 GEORGE FOSTER No one who ever saw George Foster would accuse him of taking steroids—even after he hit 52 home runs for Cincinnati in 1977. Weighing just 185 pounds, Foster hit home runs the Hank Aaron way—all wrists and technique. After he ended his career with 348 round trips around the bases in 18 seasons, he looked back and said, "The strong point in my life has been letting Christ be in control. He's the way, the truth, and the life."

23. BATTING PRACTICE

"I have come that they may have life, and have it to the full."
JOHN 10:10

One of the coolest things about attending a major league baseball game is getting to the ballpark early for batting practice. It's great to watch your favorite players crank a few balls over the fence. For the baseball purists left out there, it's a must experience. The average fan can take it or leave it. For them, it is a mere formality before the real game begins. But for those of us who think Opening Day should replace New Year's Day in importance, batting practice is a grand exhibition.

FAST FACT:

One of the coolest "batting practice" pitchers was 71-year-old Clay Council, who pitched batting practice to Josh Hamilton when he was a kid. Hamilton picked him to throw to him during the 2008 Home Run Derby at Yankee Stadium.

I sometimes wonder if we view life on this earth as batting practice—as just a routine formality we have to go through as we wait to get to the real action: heaven.

Make no mistake about it. Heaven is going to be one thrilling adventure! We will be reunited with those in Christ who have gone before us (1 Thessalonians 4:13–14). Jesus is going to give us creation back the way it was originally meant to be (Revelation 21:5). And together, we will expand on "the kingdom" prepared for us "since the creation of the world" (Matthew 25:34).

Yes, heaven is really good news! But let's not forget another part of the good news. When Jesus said that He came to give us life, He wasn't talking about some little bitty life with no value. He said He came to give us life "to the full" (John 10:10). That is life now!

Our life before heaven isn't like batting practice. We are not simply going through the motions or gutting out some painful losses before the real game begins. The real game is already underway. Are you going to play, or just stand there?

—JEFF OLSON

FOLLOW THROUGH

Start asking, seeking, and knocking for more of the "life" God is offering (Luke 11:9–13).

For Further Reading: Read the book *Waking the Dead* by John Eldredge.

NO. 23 AL OLIVER Not many people hit a baseball with as much authority as Al Oliver. Others have more hits or more home runs or more Hall of Fame votes, but few could scold the leather like Scoop. When he was done spraying frozen ropes around the majors between 1968 and 1985, he had 2,743 hits; 1,326 RBI; and a .303 average. Though many can't understand why those aren't Cooperstown numbers, Oliver is philosophical: "I'll join my parents in God's Hall of Fame where everybody will be on the same playing field."

24. MARSHMALLOW CHRISTIANS

Strike Zone:
Training spiritually

"Run in such a way as to get the prize."
1 CORINTHIANS 9:24

When closer Bobby Jenks showed up at the Chicago White Sox' spring training camp one season packing a few extra pounds, manager Ozzie Guillen didn't take the view that bigger was better. So he began having daily meetings with Jenks.

"I told him when you show up out of shape, you're ruining 25 guys wearing this uniform," Guillen said. "You're not ruining myself or you, you're ruining your teammates."

Three spiritual applications become clear: 1. We can't afford to neglect our spiritual training; 2. Everything we do reflects either positively or negatively on our fellow believers and on Jesus Christ; 3. None of us can do it alone. We need a "manager"—an accountability partner to ask us hard questions.

FAST FACT:
Bobby Jenks packs his 270 pounds into a 6-3 frame. By contrast, Babe Ruth, who was 6-2, weighed 215 pounds.

Physical conditioning is difficult but essential work if we want to be winners in athletics. But how do we keep from becoming spiritual marshmallows? Here are a few training tips: Establish a daily time to read God's Word and pray. Make this your No. 1 priority! Set realistic goals. Don't set out to read the entire Bible if you haven't been reading it at all. Don't try to pray for a half-hour if you can only concentrate for two or three minutes. Keep a journal and record your prayer requests, answers to prayer, and praises. Use a devotional guide such as *Our Daily Bread* or *My Utmost for His Highest* to keep you motivated. Get an accountability partner to help you keep at it.

The apostle Paul instructed us to go into "strict training" for our spiritual health (1 Corinthians 9:25). If we establish a plan and stick to it, success is not only possible, it's inevitable. Consistency is crucial if you want to avoid becoming a marshmallow Christian.

—TIM GUSTAFSON

FOLLOW THROUGH

When is the best time for you to read your Bible? Is it easier for you to write down prayer requests in a notebook? Blackberry? Laptop? Think of a person who could best help you as an accountability partner.

From the Playbook: Read 1 Corinthians 9:24–27.

NO. 24 RICK AGUILERA It's easy to forget that big-time baseball players have their ups and downs. During a down time for Aguilera, he rededicated his life to Jesus. "I was wondering where I was headed. I said, 'Lord, I don't know where my life is going. You can have it. Help me to follow you wholeheartedly and put you first.'" Aggie finished with 318 saves and an ERA of 3.57.

25. WHO CALLS THE GAME?

*"Will the one who contends with the
Almighty correct him?"*

JOB 40:2

During an afternoon baseball game back in the 1920s, American League umpire Bill Guthrie was working behind home plate, and the catcher for the visiting team repeatedly protested his calls.

According to a story in the *St. Louis Post Dispatch*, Guthrie endured the complaining for three innings. But in the fourth inning, when the catcher started to protest again, Guthrie stopped him. "Son," he said gently, "you've been a big help to me calling balls and strikes, and I appreciate it. But I think I've got the hang of it now. So I'm going to ask you to go to the clubhouse and show them how to take a shower."

FAST FACT:
*Bill Guthrie
umpired in the
National League
in 1913 and 1915
and in the Ameri-
can League from
1928–1932.*

Job also had been complaining about calls he didn't think were fair. In his case, the umpire was God. After listening to Job's objections, the Lord finally spoke out of a violent storm. When He did, things came into perspective for Job. God was gentle, but He was also firm and direct. The Lord asked Job the kinds of questions that bring finite man back down to size. Job listened, gave up his complaining, and found peace in surrendering to God.

"Father, we don't make sense when we complain about your fairness. Help us to be like your Son Jesus, who trusted you without complaining, even to the point of dying on the cross."

—MART DE HAAN

FOLLOW THROUGH

Which of God's dealings in your life do you complain about? What would happen if you were to turn those complaints into trust?

From the Playbook: Read: Job 40:1–14.

NO. 25 DAN QUISENBERRY From his delivery to his writing style, relief pitcher Quisenberry was quirky. Yet he knew where he was going. Even as brain cancer was robbing him of life, he kept trusting God. In one of his poems, he wrote the following:

*in the beginning was the word
and it was God,
and still is.*

The Quiz died in 1998 at age 45, just 8 years after retiring with 244 saves and a tiny ERA of 2.57.

26. FROM THE PROS TO THE PULPIT

"Always give yourselves fully to the work of the Lord, because you know that your labor in the Lord is not in vain."

1 CORINTHIANS 15:58

If you visit the Billy Graham Museum at Wheaton College in Illinois, you might be surprised to find a former professional baseball player featured as one of the most influential American evangelists of the early twentieth century.

FAST FACT:
Billy Sunday played for three National League teams: The Chicago Cubs, the Pittsburgh Pirates, and the Philadelphia Phillies.

His name is William (Billy) Ashley Sunday, and his journeys, both into professional sports and the pulpit, are fascinating. Born into poverty, Sunday grew up in an orphanage before venturing out on his own—surviving on wages from a series of odd jobs in small towns in Iowa. At that time he demonstrated prowess as an amateur athlete. Exceptionally fast, Sunday made his way to the majors where he starred for 8 years.

After converting to Christianity in the 1880s, Sunday retired from baseball and went into full-time Christian ministry. He honed his skills as a pulpit evangelist in the Midwest, and soon he became the nation's most famous evangelist with what some labeled his "colloquial sermons and frenetic delivery."

Sunday held heavily reported Christian crusades in America's largest cities, and it is believed that he may have personally preached the gospel of Jesus Christ to more people than any other person in history up to that time, with more than a million people coming forward at his invitations.

Baseball played an important chapter in Sunday's life. He knew, however, that the end of his sporting career meant an opportunity for him to engage more fully in the work of the Lord (1 Corinthians 15:58). What can we do to be more fully at work for God?

—ROXANNE ROBBINS

FOLLOW THROUGH

What does "the work of the Lord" mean to you? How will you, in the near future, do that work?

From the Playbook: Read 1 Corinthians 15:50–58.

NO. 26 DOUG JONES He was the Johnny Appleseed of saves, spreading them throughout the majors: 124 in Cleveland (1986–91); 62 in Houston (1992–93); 27 in Philadelphia ('94); 22 in Baltimore ('95); 49 in Milwaukee (1996–98); 12 in Oakland (1999–2000). Not including 1 in the 1989 All-Star Game. Of it all, he said simply, "My job is to get people out. Do it as a Christian should, as unto the Lord."

27. CALLING BALLS AND STRIKES

"Let the peace of Christ rule in your hearts, since as members of one body you were called to peace."

COLOSSIANS 3:15

I volunteered once to umpire a church softball game.

One of the biggest mistakes of my life.

My fellow brothers in the Lord let me know that I was blind, that I didn't know what a strike zone looked like, or that I couldn't recognize a check swing. Reminds me of a joke I heard once. An umpire threw a big league manager out of the game and told him to "go someplace where I can't see you anymore." He walked over and stood on home plate.

FAST FACT:

In MLB, to prevent bias behind the plate, the umpiring crew rotates each game from home, to third, second and first, then back to home plate.

We sure love to hate umpires. The devil challenged God to a baseball game. God said sure, I have the best players of all time on my team. The devil said, "Yeah, but I've got all the umpires."

Colossians 3:15 says, "Let the peace of Christ rule in your hearts." The word for rule is the word *umpire*. In other words, let Christ call the balls and strikes in your life. He's the umpire who knows what's in the zone and what isn't. Human umpires make mistakes. I know some guys in a church softball league who can verify that. But Christ will never miss a pitch. If you trust His judgment and listen to the call, His peace will fill your heart.

A little leaguer whose bat was almost as tall as he was, struck out on every trip to the plate. Finally, after the last strike out, he told the coach he just couldn't hit off this umpire.

Indeed there is only one "umpire" we can truly trust. Listen to the "balls and strikes" Christ calls, and let peace into your heart. You *can* hit off this umpire.

—DAN DEAL

FOLLOW THROUGH

Who usually rules your heart? Is it someone who is all knowing and has all-knowledge? How about entrusting those judgment calls to Jesus?

From the Playbook: Read Colossians 3:1–17 and find the true field of dreams.

NO. 27 DWIGHT EVANS As a baseball player, Evans was known as a batter with a thousand stances. He became an All-Star using his multiple batting styles. But his stance on two things never changed. His love for family showed through in his care for his son Tim, who has a serious nerve disease, and his love for life, demonstrated by his affiliation with Battin' 1.000, a pro-life group of athletes. Evans hit .272 with 385 home runs in his 20-year career.

28. OLD DUDES

"After forty years had passed, an angel appeared to Moses in the flames of a burning bush."

ACTS 7:30

In honor of Julio Franco, who played in the majors until he was 49 years old, let's talk about Old Dudes—really ancient people who did some amazing work long after their Use By date.

Before that, though, a word about Julio. When he retired in 2008, he was the only active player who had batted against a pitcher who also faced the great Ted Williams. Early in his career, Franco stood in against Jim Kaat, who pitched to Teddy Ballgame in 1960. Williams began his major league career in 1939. One pitcher he faced was Red Ruffing, who began in 1924 and pitched to Ty Cobb, who began in 1905. So Franco's appearance as a major leaguer completed a link that went back more than 100 years in the majors.

FAST FACT:
Franco is the oldest major leaguer to hit a home run and steal a base.

Abraham and Sarah definitely get into the Old Dudes Hall of Fame. They set the standard for "Accomplishing Surprising Results by a Nonagenarian" when they had baby Isaac in their tenth decade. ("Abe, do you realize that when Isaac graduates from high school, we'll be 113 years old?" Sarah may have said.) Also, Moses might be a good candidate for the Old Dudes HOF. He was 80 when at the burning bush God asked him to lead the children of Israel on a 40-year journey.

Remember, it was 80-year-old Moses who told God that He couldn't teach an old dude a new trick like leadership. Yet with God's help and enablement, Old Mo got the job done.

What's the point of all this? It's simply that no matter how old you are it's not too late to get active for God. Some people put life on cruise control at 50—others are still changing lives at 80. Which are you going to be?

—DAVE BRANON

FOLLOW THROUGH

What sounds like old to you? Do you think God keeps people around after that for a reason? Or not?

From the Playbook: Read Genesis 18:1–15 and Genesis 21:1–7.

NO. 28 JULIO FRANCO Talk about your elder statesman! Julio Franco nearly made it to 50 as a major leaguer before retiring at 49 in 2008. One thing Franco learned in his 23 years as a major leaguer was this: "Without God, I am nothing. I never was anything. I want to be faithful to God for His wonderful gifts and give back everything I can." Franco ended with 2,586 hits and the 1991 American League batting title (.341).

29. FILLED WITH ANXIETY?

"Cast all your anxiety on him because he cares for you."

1 PETER 5:7

When I played Little League baseball, I was a sweet-swinging first baseman who hit in the heart of my team's batting order. (Think John Olerud without the power. And a lot shorter.) My batting average was high, I drove in runs, and I rarely struck out.

Yet one game—specifically one at-bat—stands out in my mind to this day (more than 25 years later). It was the seventh (and final) inning of a game against our top rival.

Trailing by a run, I was the first hitter to face the opposing team's star pitcher, who they brought into this game as their closer. As I stood in the on-deck circle and watched his fastball buzz toward home plate, I was overwhelmed with emotion. Each time he let loose a warm-up pitch, the catcher's mitt would crack—and so would my confidence. By the time I stepped in against this 11-year-old Nolan Ryan-wannabe, I was filled with anxiety. I had become so riddled with fear that my only goal was not to get hit by one of his heaters.

FAST FACT:
The official Little League was founded by Carl Stotz in Williamsport, Pennsylvania, in 1939.

I didn't get hit. But I didn't get a hit either. I grounded out weakly.

My Little League at-bat is similar to the way many of us live out our faith. We become so anxiety-filled, so fear-stricken of the challenges in our lives that we lose sight of the reality of the One who is carefully orchestrating all of life. The God we serve cares for us more deeply than we could ever imagine. The best way to face anxiety is to trust Him with our fears and let Him carry the burden. He truly cares.

—Rob Bentz

FOLLOW THROUGH

Through prayer, ask God to comfort you and give you peace over the challenges that are currently causing you anxiety and fear.

From the Playbook: Read 1 Peter 5:1–11.

NO. 29 JOHN OLERUD A brain aneurysm nearly killed Olerud when he was 20, but he recovered to enjoy a stellar major league career. Equipped with his ever-present batting helmet (even on defense) to protect his head, Olerud hit .295 in a 17-year career highlighted by a .363 batting average in 1993. He became a Christian after his brush with mortality and after his future wife, Kelly, led him to faith.

30. A GOOD WIFE

It is not good for the man to be alone. I will make a helper suitable for him."

GENESIS 2:18

My wife Alicia is just right for me. I'm so thankful to have her as my wife and the mother of our daughter, Reagan. Alicia is such a help and encouragement to me every day. I don't know what I would do without her.

I started dating Alicia while we were in college at the University of Kentucky, and she supported me the whole way. I always had dreams and aspirations of playing major league baseball, and she never doubted me. She never said, "Just go get your college education, and then try and play baseball." She never said anything like that, which could have deterred me from pursuing my dream. She was always pushing me to go out there and give it my best in my drive to be drafted and play in the majors.

FAST FACT:
Alicia's father, who helped Brandon with his offseason baseball camps, died in December 2005.

God knew what He was doing when He made a "helper" for Adam way back there in the Garden of Eden . . . and He knew what he was doing when He brought Alicia and me together. She backs me up in everything I do.

One example of a time Alicia and I felt God showed us the value of our relationship was 2006—a wild and crazy year. We suffered two deaths of people close to us, we rejoiced in the birth of Reagan, and we celebrated a Cy Young Award. I needed Alicia in order to make it.

It's awesome to have someone alongside you—helping you through it. Guys, praise God for the suitable helper (Genesis 2:18) He has provided you.

—BRANDON WEBB

FOLLOW THROUGH

Schedule a date night and tell your spouse how much you appreciate him or her.

From the Playbook: Meditate on Proverbs 18:22.

NO. 30 BRANDON WEBB Just six seasons into his major league career, Webb already had 85 wins and two Cy Young Awards—and a 16-loss season. He bounced back from a 7-16 second year to win 68 games in the next four seasons. Yet he knows that life is not baseball. "Anybody who knows God knows that baseball is an extracurricular thing. He's got more important things for us to do than just play baseball. The biggest thing He has for us to do is to spread His Word."

31. THE BIBLE TELLS ME SO

*"Do not let this Book of the Law depart from your mouth;
meditate on it day and night."*

JOSHUA 1:8

For this spiritual lesson from the world of baseball, do something different. Be challenged and encouraged by reading and meditating on Bible verses that a variety of players—active and retired—have said are particularly meaningful in their personal walk with Christ.

- Garrett Anderson, outfielder: "A gentle answer turns away wrath" (Proverbs 15:1).
- Scott Linebrink, relief pitcher: "Whatever you do, work at it with all your heart, as working for the Lord, not for men" (Colossians 3:23).
- Kyle Abbott, pitcher: "Cast all your anxiety on him because he cares for you" (1 Peter 5:7).
- Mike Sweeney, first baseman: "Though you have not seen him, you love him; and even though you do not see him now, you believe in him and are filled with an inexpressible and glorious joy, for you are receiving the goal of your faith, the salvation of your souls" (1 Peter 1:8–9).
- Jake Peavy, pitcher: "'For I know the plans I have for you,' declares the LORD, 'plans to prosper you and not to harm you, plans to give you hope and a future'" (Jeremiah 29:11).

FAST FACT:

The verse that is most often cited by athletes as their favorite is Philippians 4:13.

74

- Gary Knotts, pitcher: "It is God who arms me with strength and makes my way perfect" (Psalm 18:32).
- Russ Ortiz, pitcher: "And the peace of God, which transcends all understanding, will guard your hearts and your minds in Christ Jesus" (Philippians 4:7).

Each of these players can readily explain the value of Scripture in their lives. What about you? Can you point people to Bible verses and passages that have helped you know Christ better? Take a note from Joshua: Meditate on the Word.

—ROXANNE ROBBINS

FOLLOW THROUGH

On a 3 x 5 card, write down a Bible verse that is important to you. Carry it throughout the week and read it often. Then try making that a weekly habit.

From the Playbook: Read Joshua 1:6–9.

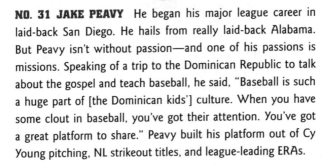

NO. 31 JAKE PEAVY He began his major league career in laid-back San Diego. He hails from really laid-back Alabama. But Peavy isn't without passion—and one of his passions is missions. Speaking of a trip to the Dominican Republic to talk about the gospel and teach baseball, he said, "Baseball is such a huge part of [the Dominican kids'] culture. When you have some clout in baseball, you've got their attention. You've got a great platform to share." Peavy built his platform out of Cy Young pitching, NL strikeout titles, and league-leading ERAs.

32. CAN YOU TOP CAL RIPKEN?

Well done, good and faithful servant! You have been faithful with a few things; I will put you in charge of many things."

MATTHEW 25:23

Two-thousand, six-hundred, and thirty-two consecutive games.

Just imagine showing up to play baseball that many games in a row—never taking a rest over the course of 16 years despite injury, fatigue, and baseball's ups and downs.

That's what Baltimore Orioles shortstop Cal Ripken Jr. did between 1983 and 1998, showing up to work without fail to break Lou Gehrig's 56-year-old record for longevity—a record many thought would never be broken. The reward? A place in the Baseball Hall of Fame.

FAST FACT:

Lou Gehrig's string of games began after Yankees regular first baseman Wally Pipp told his manager he would like a day off.

Pretty dependable, right?

Not as dependable as someone who walks faithfully with God every day. Of course, there's no record for remaining loyal in our Christian walk, but Jesus has entrusted us with certain gifts that He expects us to use as we serve Him consistently.

In Matthew, Jesus told a parable about a master who entrusted some money to three servants. Two of the servants turned their gifts into more while the third hid his allotment and returned with what he was given. The first two were rewarded for making their gifts profitable while the third was scolded for not doing anything.

Just as Ripken multiplied his baseball talent year after year through his diligence, so God expects us to take what He has given to us and transform it into something special. With perseverance and faithfulness, use your God-given gifts consistently for His glory. You won't be sorry you did.

—JEFF ARNOLD

FOLLOW THROUGH

Take time today to think of something God has entrusted to you, and ask Jesus to help you be faithful and turn it into something extraordinary.

From the Playbook: Read Matthew 25:14–28.

NO. 32. FRANK TANANA Tanana had two careers: one as a fireballing, hard-living playboy and one as a finesse-pitching, clean-living Christian. An injury to his arm changed his pitching style. An encounter with the Savior altered his life. He won 240 games in a 21-year career and then moved into a role as a respected Christian gentleman who mentors men and loves to tell how Jesus changed his life.

33. REAL COMMITMENT

Believe in the Lord Jesus, and you will be saved."

Acts 16:31

I have learned a lot since making my major league debut in 1998. Developing the skills necessary to hit major league pitching while learning the pitching staff well enough to be an effective, everyday catcher has not come easily. However, I have been committed to improving myself every day.

Another area of my life that I have dedicated myself to over the past few years has been understanding what a real commitment to Jesus Christ means. While I grew up going to church and understood what it meant to have a personal relationship with Christ, it took me a long time to commit my life to Him and to live for Him.

FAST FACT:
Michael's cousin, Scott Fletcher, had a 15-year major league career.

Every day is a learning process, and each day is filled with its own challenges. It is my goal to please the Lord out of love for Him and gratitude for eternal life. It is great to know that because I placed my trust in Jesus Christ alone for my salvation I am assured of spending eternity in heaven. There is nothing I could ever do that could earn this—for salvation is a free gift from God, who sent His Son to die on the cross in my place. "For the wages of sin is death, but the gift of God is eternal life in Christ Jesus our Lord" (Romans 6:23).

Knowing Christ and walking with Him each day, reading the Bible and praying—these give my life meaning and allow me to live with joy, not regret. These are the grand results of true commitment to my Savior.

I hope you have an eternal relationship with Jesus Christ. He is the only way to the Father. Jesus said, "I am the way and the truth and the life. No one comes to the Father except through me" (John 14:6). Are you ready to commit?

—MICHAEL BARRETT

FOLLOW THROUGH

Do you know Jesus the way Michael described? Trusting Jesus as Savior is the most important thing you can do on this earth. Please trust Him today.

For Further Reading: Read the booklet *Do I Have the Right Kind of Faith?* Go to www.discoveryseries.org/q0603.

33 MATT HOLLIDAY It wasn't exactly a breakout season for Holliday in 2007 when he hit .340 with 36 home runs and 137 RBI. He had already been over .300 twice and over the 100 RBI mark. But his team, the Colorado Rockies, did break out to go to the World Series. Holliday came "this close" to being the NL MVP. And he got to show the world his faith, saying, "I build relationships and prepare my heart for a chance to share with others. God will use me in a way that will glorify Him."

34. CHECK YOUR SWING

Plans fail for lack of counsel, but with many
advisors they succeed."

PROVERBS 15:22

He is regarded by many as the top offensive catcher of all time, and he holds the career record for home runs hit by a catcher. In 1997 Mike Piazza hit .362, the highest batting average for any catcher in more than 50 years, and he racked up a slugging percentage of .638. With 40 homers, 124 RBIs, 104 runs, and 201 hits, Piazza had the greatest offensive season of any catcher in more than 100 years. Now, that's impressive!

FAST FACT:

Mike Piazza was drafted in the 62nd round of the 1988 Major League Baseball draft. He was the 1,390th player chosen that year.

So, when Piazza gives advice about the fundamentals of batting, we should pay attention! Here are a few of his tips:

1. Stay inside of the ball so you can hit it to all fields.
2. Hold your bat at a 45-degree angle to alleviate unnecessary movement in your swing.
3. Keep your back elbow close to your body to help your hands and the barrel of the bat swing through the ball.
4. Have someone watch you while you swing and check your mechanics.

That fourth tip can come in handy in our faith life. Many times the only way to improve our walk with Jesus is to have someone observe us and check our mechanics. Proverbs 15:22 says, "Plans fail for lack of counsel, but with many advisers they succeed." Perhaps you need someone in your life who is willing to check your mechanics and tell you if your fundamentals need to be sharpened.

Are you practicing the basics of the Christian faith? Find someone who will honestly critique your "mechanics" to see if you can connect with Jesus in a deeper and more profound way.

—MOLLY RAMSEYER

FOLLOW THROUGH

Make a list of two or three people who could be potential accountability partners for you. Make a point to give one of them a call to discuss it.

From the Playbook: Read Mark 9 to discover whom Jesus chose as His closest confidants.

NO. 34 CARLOS ZAMBRANO While the Chicago Cubs were still struggling toward respectability in the early 2000s, Big Z toiled away—winning double-digits each year. In eight seasons, he reached 100 victories and fanned more than 1200 batters. Zambrano knows he has something special in his magical right arm. "When God gives you something, you have to hold onto it hard. God gave me the ability to play in the big leagues, and you have to do your part and do it the best you can."

35. OFFENSIVE UNIFORMS

"We long to put on our heavenly bodies like new clothing."
2 CORINTHIANS 5:2 (NLT)

Could a baseball club's best offense be its uniforms? A team from Paducah, Kentucky, would have said, "Yes."

As documented in the book *Three Men on Third: A Book of Baseball Anecdotes, Oddities, and Curiosities,* "The Paducahs were competing in a Kentucky-Indiana-Tennessee League game against Mayfield in 1936. Due to a mix-up, the Paducahs' uniforms were not given their usual pre-game washing. The team played in dirty uniforms and won anyway, 13-4."

FAST FACT:
Paducah played 23 seasons in the Kentucky-Indiana-Tennessee League.

Because they won, the team decided to keep playing in their dirty duds. But as the weeks and *months* passed, opposing infielders didn't even try to keep Paducah base runners close to their respective bags due to the offensive odor. Catchers, in particular, were sickened by the stench when Paducah was up to bat.

But playing smelly paid off for the Kentuckians, for they ended up capturing the league championship while still wearing their "ripe" clothing!

Our current "clothing," as the apostle Paul wrote in 2 Corinthians 5, will one day give way to new clothing—our heavenly bodies (v. 2). This is a not a negative view of the remarkable bodies God has given us, but it is a reminder of the great hope we can have in God's plan for our future!

Paul recognized that his physical body was gradually breaking down (4:16). His perspective was eternal, however, as he focused on what his new body would be like in heaven.

You may be perfectly healthy, or you may have some serious health challenges. In either situation, as a believer in Jesus, you will one day be wearing "new clothes" in His presence.

You can have great confidence and joy as you anticipate eternity with Him!

—TOM FELTEN

FOLLOW THROUGH

Take five minutes and think about the health challenges that God has led you and others close to you through. What have you learned about God through the frailty of our bodies? How does it make you feel to know that you will have "new clothes" in His presence one day?

From the Playbook: Read 2 Corinthians 5:1–8.

NO. 35 MARK LANGSTON In four of his first five seasons as a major league pitcher, Mark Langston struck out more than 200 hitters. Twice in that span, he led the AL in strikeouts as he anchored the Seattle Mariners' staff. Before he was done, the lefty from San Diego had gotten three strikes past 2,464 hitters, putting him in the Top 30 all-time. Langston was named to four All-Star teams, and he picked up seven Gold Gloves for his fielding prowess. After retiring, he coached high school baseball at Orange County Lutheran High School, where his kids attended.

36. A BASEBALL LETTER

*You show that you are a letter from Christ,
the result of our ministry."*

2 CORINTHIANS 3:3

Relief pitcher Todd Jones, once dubbed "The Roller Coaster" by Tigers Hall of Fame broadcaster Ernie Harwell, is Detroit's all-time saves leader. Jones has won the American League Rolaids Relief Man Award. He has been a major league All-Star. He is one of only 21 pitchers in the history of baseball to register 300 or more saves in his career.

FAST FACT:

Jones recorded his 200th save as a Tiger on July 4, 2007.

Yet Jones acknowledges that his success as a big league closer is due to one man—former Detroit manager Buddy Bell. Bell was the Tigers' skipper when the team acquired Jones, then a set-up man, from the Houston Astros prior to the 1997 season. Jones told the *Detroit Free Press*, "He taught me how to close games when I didn't know how to close. He's a great man."

Even after Bell's managing career in the big leagues was over, his legacy lived on through Todd Jones.

In the New Testament, the apostle Paul made a similar acknowledgment in his second letter to the church in Corinth. He reminded the church leaders of his ministry in their midst. Paul reminded them of the power of the transformed lives they had witnessed. He reminded them of the significant work God had done in the Corinthian church through his ministry. They were his "letter from Christ" for the world to see!

God uses key people in our lives to bring about transformation. In the baseball life of Todd Jones that person was Buddy Bell. Who is that person in your life? Thank God for giving you a "letter from Christ."

—Rob Bentz

FOLLOW THROUGH

In prayer, thank God for the person who has written a letter on your heart. Ask God to bring someone into your life He can use you for in the same manner.

From the Playbook: Read and mediate on 2 Corinthians 3:1–6.

NO. 36 TODD JONES The facts speak for themselves. In a career that spanned 16 seasons, Todd Jones appeared in nearly a thousand games—all but one of them in relief—and made one All-Star team, won the AL Rolaids Relief Award, led the league in saves, and pitched in the World Series. He racked up more than 300 saves and wrote a column for *The Sporting News*. He pitched for Team USA in the World Baseball Classic. He was the last pitcher ever to pitch at Tiger Stadium. But above all, he says, "I just need to believe in Jesus as my Savior."

37. A BETTER PERSON

Strike Zone:
Finding hope in tragedy

"We do not want you to be uninformed, brothers, about the hardships we suffered . . . This happened that we might not rely on ourselves but on God."

2 CORINTHIANS 1:8–9

Vicki Schmidt died of a brain tumor in April 2003. The hundreds of people who gathered for her funeral sounded a common theme: She was a person who was devoted to her family and to Christ. As her son, major league pitcher Jason Schmidt, sat listening to the tributes, he was flooded with emotions. He began to reflect on what matters most in life.

FAST FACT: *Between 1997 and 2006, Jason Schmidt won at least 10 games every season but one.*

Schmidt, who by then had established himself as one of the top pitchers in the game during his years with Pittsburgh and San Francisco, realized that his mom's death would make a change in who he was.

"People are always going to remember me for baseball," he says. "Is that really the real reason we're here? I would like to be remembered as a Christian athlete. When we pass away, what are people going to say? Are they going to know what we stood for? They're gonna know when I pass away where I'm going. That's the No. 1 thing."

Understandably, the death proved difficult for Schmidt, his family, and his friends. "That was a hard phone call to make," says fellow major league pitcher and brother in Christ Russ Ortiz, who phoned his friend just after Mrs. Schmidt's death. "He's such a good friend that I couldn't help but start crying."

If there is any silver lining in this dark cloud, Ortiz says he thinks Schmidt's mother's death actually made Jason a stronger Christian. "When your perspective and your priority is Jesus, whatever happens you know you can still get through it. And it seems to me, that's where he's at," Ortiz says of Schmidt. "He's become a better person and a better player because of everything he's gone through."

When tough things happen to us, are we willing to let those difficulties make us a better person?

—MARK MORAN

FOLLOW THROUGH

Can this really happen? Can truly bad news—tragic news—somehow make you into a better person? This can happen only if you allow God to shape you and use you. Has it ever happened with you? How?

From the Playbook: Read 2 Corinthians 1:1–10.

NO. 37 JASON SCHMIDT He started his career as a member of the vaunted Atlanta Braves' pitching staff in the mid 1990s—but Schmidt's best years were with the San Francisco Giants. Between 2002 and 2005, he won 60 games for the Giants and helped them get to the 2002 World Series. Injuries limited him after that—and drove him to the Bible. "I was at my wit's end. I started reading my Bible, and everything just made sense. I couldn't wait to read the Bible. It changed my life."

38. LIVING A LIE

*"Woe to you, teachers of the law and Pharisees,
you hypocrites!"*

MATTHEW 23:13

On June 28, 1969, Bill Henry was released by the Houston Astros, ending a lengthy major league career that began in 1952. As a kid, Henry was discovered by a scout who saw him pitching in a fast-pitch softball league. He had a good career, but he wasn't surprised by the news that the Astros were cutting him loose.

He *was* surprised one day in 2007, though, by the news that he had passed away. A baseball historian called his wife to offer condolences after reading of his death at the Lakeland (FL) Medical Center.

FAST FACT:
Bill Henry represented the Cincinnati Reds in the 1960 All-Star Game.

"Bill didn't pass away in Florida," she told the caller from their Texas home. "He's sitting here next to me."

As it turns out, the Bill Henry who died of a heart attack in Florida was not the Bill Henry who accumulated 90 saves while wearing six different uniforms. He only said he was. The copycat Bill Henry—actually a retired salesman from Michigan—told his wife and stepchildren and anyone who would listen that he was a former major league pitcher, with baseball cards (the real baseball-playing Bill Henry's, of course) to prove it.

"I was married to a man maybe I didn't know," his widow marveled.

That's an extreme example of a fundamental problem we all struggle with—being who we say we are.

Jesus' most stinging words of rebuke spoke to the hypocrisy of the Pharisees (Matthew 23). Later, in the early days of the church, God's judgment on Ananias and Sapphira also signaled how serious it is to try to impress others with phony "spirituality."

Living a lie is not something God takes lightly.

—BRIAN HETTINGA

FOLLOW THROUGH

Famous preacher Charles Haddon Spurgeon believed that the best cure for hypocrisy is to remember that no matter where we are, God is with us. We never really do anything in secret. He doesn't fall for our lies.

From the Playbook: Read Acts 5:1–11.

NO. 38 CARL ERSKINE One of the "Boys of Summer," Erskine played in the golden era when the Dodgers and Giants were still in Brooklyn and New York (he did end his career in 1959 after the Dodgers moved to LA). He won 122 games for the Bums, and he got to pitch in five World Series. The father of a special needs son, Erskine helped develop the Hopewell Center in his hometown of Anderson, Indiana, to help kids like his son Jimmy. He also was a charter member of the Fellowship of Christian Athletes.

39. BEST IN THE LEAGUE?

Strike Zone:
Trusting God with your life

But I trust in you, O Lord; I say, 'You are my God.'
My times are in your hands."

PSALM 31:14–15

Amazing! I had been drafted by the Chicago Cubs, and my path to stardom was right in front of me. Although I hadn't thought much about playing baseball in the big leagues before, when I was drafted I was enthralled with thoughts of all the riches and recognition I might enjoy.

FAST FACT:
Shawn's best year in the majors was 1996, when he was 12-11 for the Los Angeles Angels.

As do most baseball players, I toiled in the minor leagues for a while, working my way up. After four years in the minors, the call came. I was headed to "The Show."

During my first years in the majors, I had mixed results, so I was starting to get frustrated. I talked things over with sports psychologist John Niednagel, bemoaning my inconsistency on the field. After all, all I wanted was to be the best player in the league—and it wasn't happening.

Niednagel said something that has stuck with me ever since. "Shawn," he began, "What would it take for God to make you a five-time Cy Young Award winner?" I knew the answer: Nothing more than the snap of God's fingers.

We athletes want to be the best. However, the more we concentrate on an award or success in general, the more likely we are to miss it. Success, like happiness, cannot be pursued; it must ensue. In other words, it must follow from God's hand.

And it does this only as the by-product of our surrender to a person other than ourselves, namely, Jesus. Author John Ortberg has observed, "True joy comes only to those who have devoted themselves to something greater than personal happiness." And that devotion must be to our Savior.

Sure, we should strive to be the best we can be, but God alone gives the increase (1 Corinthians 3:6–7). Our job is to keep our eyes fixed on the Author and Perfecter of our faith. Any success we enjoy comes from the One who truly holds all our "times" in His hand.

—SHAWN BOSKIE

FOLLOW THROUGH

What goals have you set that you are striving too hard to accomplish, forgetting that your times are in God's hands, not yours? What would be some better goals—ones that will glorify God, not you?

From the Playbook: Read Psalm 33:6–11.

NO. 39 BRETT BUTLER Is he more famous for his baseball prowess or for beating cancer? Both are key elements of Butler's story. As a major leaguer, Butler lashed out 2,375 hits for the Braves, Indians, Giants, Dodgers, and Mets in a 17-year career. But it was when Butler came back from throat cancer that his legacy was solidified. "I always appreciated life and the ability God gave me to play baseball, but I take each day as this may be my last."

Store up for yourselves treasures in heaven . . . For where your treasure is, there your heart will be also."

MATTHEW 6:20–21

The Atlanta Braves spare no expense when trying to optimize a player's production. They are one of a few teams in baseball that hire a doctor to come into spring training to help hitters train and strengthen their eyes.

I am not one to jump at the opportunity to try new things, so I was skeptical. Dr. Harrison held out a dotted piece of cardboard and asked if I could see the letter in it, and indeed I could. But as he got farther away, all I could see were the dots on the card. They all blurred together. His diagnosis? I had limited depth perception after a certain distance.

FAST FACT:
Matt hit .338 for the Atlanta Braves in 2007 in 358 at bats.

Dr. Harrison quickly deduced that my right eye was lacking in strength, and this led to the problem. I was fitted with a contact lens for the right eye, and I immediately noticed a difference while playing defense. The best way I can describe it was that it used to look as if I was looking at a movie screen when I'd stand in the outfield, and now things look more three-dimensional.

Playing defense is not the only area of my life that needs depth perception. I continually live as though this life is all there is. I buy new things and am shocked when they wear out. I worry about stuff that has no eternal significance.

God is calling me . . . and you, to see things differently—to have a perception that helps us see past today and to focus on things that are eternal. He wants us to put some depth in our perception of the life He has given us.

—MATT DIAZ

FOLLOW THROUGH

What are your goals? How many of them involve an eternal perspective? What are some goals with an eternal significance that you could make more of a priority?

From the Playbook: Read 1 John 2:15–17 and answer these questions: What happens to things of the world? What happens to the man who is focused on God and His will?

NO. 40 VERN LAW Talk about old school. Vernon Law—the Preacher as some called him—pitched for 16 seasons for the same team, the Pittsburgh Pirates. Along the way, he enjoyed a remarkable year in 1960 when he won 20 games during the season and then two more in the World Series. He captured the Cy Young Award that year. When he hung up his glove, he had compiled a 162-147 record and a 3.77 ERA. Known for his faith, he said this about witnessing in a book called *The Goal and the Glory:* "One kind word spoken at the right time to the right person can result in a changed life. No disciple is exempt."

41. WHEN PAIN HURTS

"When I kept silent, my bones wasted away through my groaning all day long."

PSALM 32:3

In 2002, fans were angered when baseball's All-Star Game ended in a tie because . . . they ran out of pitchers! Contrast that dissatisfying conclusion with the dramatic finish to the 12-inning All-Star Game in 1970, when Pete Rose scored the game-winner in a seismic collision with catcher Ray Fosse. Rose later compared it to running into "a mountain."

But the mountain was mortal. Initial X-rays failed to reveal the fracture in Fosse's shoulder. He continued to play, damaged it further, and never fully recovered.

FAST FACT:

In 1970, Ray Fosse had 16 home runs before the All-Star Game and only two after it.

In life, it's often necessary to play through pain. Bad things happen to us all the time—in our jobs, in our health, in our relationships. And though it may not be healthy to wear our emotions on our sleeve, neither is it wise to pretend things are okay when they're not.

When his newborn son lay dying, David understood it was right to bare his raw emotions before the Lord. He stopped everything to fast and pray for the infant (2 Samuel 12:15–18). Later, when his son Absalom died, David was inconsolable. "O my son Absalom!" he anguished. "My son, my son Absalom. If only I had died instead of you!" (18:33). Although David's advisors chided him for the vocal intensity of his grief (19:5–7), God didn't.

The Psalms are praises to God, but they're so much more than that. They're the edgy poetry of the day, full of the angst of the ages, dripping with fear and rage and sorrow. Their conclusion, however, is deeply satisfying. "Praise be to the Lord," wrote David, "for he has heard my cry for mercy" (28:6).

—TIM GUSTAFSON

FOLLOW THROUGH

What do you do when something bad happens to you? Is your reaction healthy? Do you have a trustworthy and God-fearing friend you can turn to? Have you ever read the Psalms when you were struggling emotionally?

From the Playbook: Read Psalm 28:1–9.

NO. 41 GARRETT ANDERSON The problem with guys like Garrett Anderson is that they are so quiet. While we don't like the braggadocio of so many athletes, at least we pay attention to them. Anderson is a stealth athlete—just doing his job and not making a fuss. He deserves honor for that—and for his stellar career. Year after year, Anderson would bang out 190 or so hits, bat .290 or so, and knock in 105 runs or so. Characteristically, Anderson chose Proverbs 15:1 as his favorite verse: "A gentle answer turns away wrath."

42. YOUR DEFINING MOMENT

Strike Zone.
Serving Jesus

*I tell you the truth, wherever the gospel is preached
throughout the world, what [the woman of Bethany]
has done will also be told, in memory of her."*

MARK 14:9

Picture for a moment Joe Carter, leaping his way around the
base paths as he makes his way in celebration toward home
plate. He has just hit a Mitch Williams pitch over the fence—
winning the 1993 World Series for the Toronto Blue Jays over
the Philadelphia Phillies.

FAST FACT:

*Carter's blast was
the last World
Series action for
two years. There
was no Series in
1994 because of
a labor dispute
in baseball.*

For Carter, who had an outstanding career
with several teams, that World Series walk-off
home run became his defining moment. For
the rest of his life, that frozen point in time
will stand in the memory of every baseball fan
who hears his name.

At the same time, that slice of baseball history also became the defining moment for Williams. Despite his highly successful career as a
relief pitcher, Williams' hallmark will always
be his surrender of Carter's blast. Sadly for
him, his defining moment is marked by a disastrous finish of
the 1993 season for the Philadelphia Phillies.

Defining moments. Curt Schilling pitching for Boston
while his own personal red sock showed the pain he was
enduring to help his team break an 84-year championship
drought. Josh Hamilton hitting blast after blast into the Yankee Stadium night during the greatest Home Run Derby power

display ever. Justin Verlander jumping into Pudge Rodriguez' arms after pitching a no-hitter.

The woman of Bethany in Mark 14 had a defining moment when she anointed Jesus with expensive perfume. As Jesus predicted, her sacrifice is still remembered 2,000 years later.

What is your defining moment? What will people remember you by in your life of faith? Will it be doing a good deed for someone else? Will it be standing in the place of others in prayer? Whatever it is, if it comes from a heart of service for Christ, it'll be a moment worth remembering.

—DAVE BRANON

FOLLOW THROUGH

When people think about you and your walk of faith, what do you think they would see as your defining moment? Is there some act of service for the Lord that you would like to do as your legacy?

From the Playbook: Read Mark 14:1–9.

NO. 42 JOE CARTER Bill Mazeroski. Joe Carter. They alone ended the World Series with come-from-behind, walk-off home runs. Maz in 1960. Carter in 1993. But that wasn't all Carter did. He hit 396 home runs and accumulated 1,445 RBI in a career marked by five All-Star selections. Carter maintained humility, saying, "There's nothing great about Joe Carter and there won't be until Christ comes back."

43. FEELING FAINT?

Strike Zone:
Overcoming weariness

"Let us not become weary in doing good, for at the proper time we will reap a harvest if we do not give up."

GALATIANS 6:9

If we faint, we don't reap.

The apostle Paul, while writing to the people of Galatia, gives them one of God's life applications in chapter 6.

Many times as an athlete, I found myself growing weary and tired from the grind of it all. The rigors of training, the length of the major league baseball season, and constantly maintaining a high level of concentration and intensity needed for competition can all take their toll. The same is true of people in all professions or activities, including those who are attending school.

FAST FACT:
Fletcher finished his 15-year major league career with 1,376 hits.

So, how do we handle it all? God teaches us a valuable lesson for success in this passage from the apostle. Our Lord is telling us that maintaining our passion, energy, and zeal is very important if we want to reap the desired results. If we don't allow ourselves to grow weary, faint, and give up, there will be a harvest of great rewards awaiting us.

In other words, God, through the writing of Paul, is teaching us to stay mentally tough. Feeling faint? Press ahead. Don't give up. Reap a harvest.

—SCOTT FLETCHER

FOLLOW THROUGH

What activity are you involved in that makes you grow weary? What does it mean, "become weary in doing good"? How can you avoid doing that? What reward do you wish to receive from your hard work?

From the Playbook: Read Galatians 6:1–10.

NO. 43 TIM SALMON When injuries ended Tim Salmon's career in 2006, he was just one home run away from 300. To show how much he was appreciated in Anaheim, where he played his entire career, groundskeepers mowed his name into the outfield grass. But Salmon couldn't get No. 300. He ended with 299 HRs and 1,674 hits. And this thought: "I need to keep my eyes on God and pray for guidance and look for opportunities to glorify Him."

44. WHOSE MEASURING STICK?

*God will redeem my life from the grave;
he will surely take me to himself."*

PSALM 49:15

When he pitched, former major league lefty Mike Maroth would carve the letters F.R.O.G. in the dirt behind the mound: **F**ully **R**elying **O**n **G**od.

If he relies on God so much, why has Maroth so often met with hardship? In the dismal 2003 season, he became the first 20-game loser since 1980. When his Detroit Tigers finally broke a 12-year losing skid with a trip to the World Series in 2006, he was injured and missed the playoffs. After a trade in 2007, more arm trouble bloated his ERA and pummeled his won-loss record. In 2008, he was released by the Kansas City Royals. Is Mike not relying on God enough?

FAST FACT:
In 1974, there were five 20-game losers in the majors.

Why does a good guy like Maroth struggle while guys who stand at home plate admiring their home runs so often meet with success? Why do sports shows tend to play up self-aggrandizing behavior and ignore the quiet heroes?

Psalm 49:12–13 starkly reminds us, "Man . . . is like the beasts that perish. This is the fate of those who trust in themselves." The psalm concludes, "A man who has riches without understanding is like the beasts that perish" (v. 20). One translation renders the word *riches* as *pomp*—a good way to describe the arrogant behavior we see in some athletes.

I'm certain that God is with Mike Maroth through all his pitching woes. God's measuring stick for success is radically different from ours. And it's a success that will last eternally.

The world and those who don't recognize God's role in life may seem to have the upper edge, but fully relying on God will have its eternal rewards. And that's better than winning the Cy Young Award—by a long shot.

—TIM GUSTAFSON

FOLLOW THROUGH

Do you find yourself envying others who have "success" but little or no character? What measuring stick are you using to gauge their success? Does it need to change?

From the Playbook: Read Psalm 49:10–15.

NO. 44 TONY FERNANDEZ The irony is that while Tony Fernandez is one of the best defensive shortstops ever with a career mark of .980, many will recall the ball he missed—while playing second in the 1997 World Series for Cleveland. That miss opened the door for Florida, who won the Series. His response? "Jesus says that when disaster strikes, if your life is founded on the Rock [Jesus], it won't be shaken" (Matthew 7:24–27). "My main purpose is to serve Him, no matter what."

45. MOVING ON

"Even though I walk through the valley of the shadow of death, I will fear no evil, for you are with me."

PSALM 23:4

Sometimes we have to walk through the valley of the shadow of death. When we lose someone who is close to us, life takes on a different look as we pass through that valley. This happened to me during my fourth major league season.

In August 2006, I lost a great friend. Jon Hooker was a teammate of mine when I played baseball for the University of Kentucky. Jon and his new bride Scarlett were preparing to leave for their honeymoon the day after their wedding when things went horribly wrong. Their plane got onto the wrong runway at the Blue Grass Airport in Lexington, Kentucky, and it crashed on takeoff. Jon and Scarlett were both killed.

FAST FACT:
Against the Padres, Brandon Webb recorded an emotional victory after pitching 7 innings. He said Jon was on his mind the whole time.

I had just talked to my parents, who were at the wedding the night before. They said the ceremony was awesome. They told me it had been really, really nice.

Then I got the news about Jon and Scarlett's death. I was in total shock. I was hundreds of miles away, preparing to pitch the next day against the San Diego Padres. I really felt alone and helpless.

God gave me the strength I needed to move on. I pitched the next day in Jon's memory, and then I took some time off to go be with Jon's family. God used my wife Alicia, my parents, and others to help me through that difficult time.

Even when we walk through the valley, God is so faithful!

—Brandon Webb

FOLLOW THROUGH

Make a list of some difficult things you have had to move on from. Then pray and thank God for His faithfulness.

From the Playbook: Read all of Psalm 23 for comfort and reassurance.

NO. 45 CARLOS BELTRAN New York. The mecca of baseball? Or a black hole that sucks the life out of players? Carlos Beltran has discovered a little of both in the Big Apple. After a remarkable postseason in 2004, Beltran—the 1999 AL Rookie of the Year—moved from the Houston Astros to the New York Mets. He struggled in Year 1, but hit 41 home runs in Year 2. How did he handle the change? "I know that since God led me to New York, that I must be prepared to handle it."

46. REMEMBERED WITH FAVOR

"They replied, 'Let us start rebuilding.'
So they began this good work."

NEHEMIAH 2:18

Their first attempt failed. After 24 hours and 16 minutes, they fell short by just 44 minutes! So a year later they tried again. The small, rural town of Alliance, Nebraska, rallied some 40 players to play 84 innings of baseball to set the new Guinness World Record for the longest baseball game ever played—30 hours and 5 minutes. Now, that's what I call extra innings!

FAST FACT:

The final score after 84 innings of the longest game was 120-114.

What motivated 40 players, 145 volunteers, not to mention town fans, newspaper reporters, family, and friends to stay up all night for a baseball game? What could possibly justify one broken wrist, one pulled hamstring, and hundreds of sore muscles? The people of Alliance had one aim—to be remembered with favor.

The Old Testament character Nehemiah began as merely the cupbearer to the king of Persia. But Nehemiah wanted to accomplish something significant, so he set out on the seemingly impossible task of rebuilding the walls of Jerusalem. Despite opposition and previous failures, he rallied the high priest, the rich and poor, builders, planners, and all the citizens of Jerusalem to set this part of biblical history into motion. The story told in the Bible ends with Nehemiah saying, "Remember me with favor, O my God" (Nehemiah 13:31).

What do you want to be remembered for? Is there anything in your life worth striving for so that you might be remembered with favor? Unlikely people like Nehemiah and obscure places like Alliance, Nebraska, remind us that anyone can accomplish great things!

What great thing are you going to do for God?

—MOLLY RAMSEYER

FOLLOW THROUGH

In one sentence, write down what you most want to be remembered for. How does that line up with what God has equipped you to do for Him?

From the Playbook: Read Nehemiah 4 and consider what opposition you might be facing in the accomplishment of your dreams.

NO. 46 SCOTT McGREGOR Not many major league players become pastors after they retire, but McGregor is one who did (Others: Bill Wegman, Mark Dewey, Bill Sampen). After a career in which he won 138 games and played in two World Series for Baltimore, "The Doctor" became a youth pastor in Baltimore. Later, he rejoined Baltimore as a minor league coach.

47. THE WAITING

"Get ready to cross the Jordan River into the land I am about to give them—to the Israelites."

JOSHUA 1:2

Rich "Goose" Gossage was as intimidating a presence on the pitcher's mound as any closer in the past 30 years. Gossage, known for both his Fu Manchu mustache and his blazing fastball, was elected to the Baseball Hall of Fame in 2008.

But it wasn't Gossage's first time on the ballot. Or his second. Or even his third. Rich Gossage had been on the Hall of Fame ballot eight times without getting elected!

After his eighth year of rejection, the Colorado Springs native told his hometown newspaper, *The Gazette*, "It's out of my control, and hopefully next year it will happen. But there's nothing I can do about it."

FAST FACT:

Rich Gossage recorded 310 saves during his MLB career.

Then, just one year later, Gossage received 85.8 percent of the votes from eligible voters. That was more than enough to get the Goose in (75 percent is required for election) as the only member of the Hall of Fame Class of 2008. The Goose's wait had finally ended.

In the Scriptures, God's people—the Israelites—were forced to wait on numerous occasions. None was more significant than their 40-year sojourn in the "wilderness."

In Joshua 1, we see God's love and faithfulness to His chosen people. God kept the promises He had made to Moses. After eating manna for 40 years, God's people would finally be taken out of Egypt and into the Promised Land! Yet despite Moses' faithful leadership, he never saw the Promised Land. That leadership role was given to Joshua.

Whether in biblical times or in the twenty-first century—waiting is never easy. Patience is often necessary for God to do His work in our lives.

—ROB BENTZ

FOLLOW THROUGH

Is God forcing you to wait on something you really want right now? If so, take a few moments to journal the things you're learning about God and about yourself through the process of waiting.

From the Playbook: Read Joshua 1.

NO. 47 MIKE JACKSON Sometimes it all just comes together. For Mike Jackson, that happened in 1998. That year, pitching for Cleveland, he had 40 saves and an incredible ERA of 1.55. Jackson ended with 142 career saves—and an opportunity to pitch in the 1997 World Series. That was about the time he told a reporter, "God tells us to meditate day and night on His Word, and to pray without ceasing." Jackson retired in 2004.

The younger son got together all he had, set off for a distant country and there squandered his wealth."

LUKE 15:13

Anyone who would throw away a baseball autographed by Babe Ruth gets what he deserves.

That's exactly what a couple of Florida teenagers did a few years ago, proving once again that you don't have to be intelligent to be a thief.

The two boys, who should have been out practicing baseball, broke into a baseball card store and stole sports collectibles worth $45,000. Apparently, as they were sorting through their hot stuff, they took one look at the baseball, decided it was worthless, and threw it in a dumpster.

FAST FACT:

In 2005, a signed Babe Ruth baseball sold for $150,000.

After the boys were arrested and spilled their story, authorities rushed to the dumpster in question. It was too late. The baseball, which had been signed by Babe Ruth, had met with the same fate as banana peels, old Kleenex, and discarded milk cartons: the incinerator.

Before we are too hard on the boys for tossing out this piece of baseball history, consider other valuable things people throw out all the time.

Young people throw out their virginity in the rush for pleasure. God's will gets tossed aside because of a misconception of what brings happiness. Good health gets trashed in the pursuit of some perceived enjoyment from cigarettes, alcohol, or drugs. A growing knowledge of God gets dumped by a schedule that makes no time for God's Word.

In Luke 15, we read about the son who threw away his youth, thinking he'd enjoy the fun of the party life. Well, he may have had a few good times, but it led straight to destruction. It wasn't worth throwing away his inheritance and good name for.

Consider the value of what God has given you. Then vow not to throw it out. Don't trash the good things in life.

—DAVE BRANON

FOLLOW THROUGH

Think about your health. What is something you've been doing that is not benefiting the body God gave you? Write that thing down, vow to stop it, and put the paper in a prominent place as a reminder.

From the Playbook: Read Luke 15:11–32.

NO. 48 PAUL O'NEILL Do trades help some players? In six full seasons with home-state Cincinnati, O'Neill never hit higher than .276. In his second season with the NY Yankees, he led the league with a .359 average (strike-shortened 1994). O'Neill believed that "living a life of following Christ means giving your best in everything you do." With Cincy and NY combined, O'Neill's best included getting 2,105 career hits before putting his bat away for the last time in 2001.

49. MEET THE CHALLENGE

"Just as you received Christ Jesus as Lord, continue to live in him, rooted and built up in him."

COLOSSIANS 2:6–7

The mental and physical grind of a major league baseball season is one of the greatest challenges a ballplayer faces. The 2005 Chicago White Sox met this challenge and persevered. This team surprised the experts as they battled through adversity and injury, individual slumps, and losing streaks. They refused to believe those who said they did not have World Series potential. Rather, the Sox stuck with the fundamentals of the game and remained confident in who they were. They ended up champions.

FAST FACT:
Bryan pitched for the Giants, Cubs, and Rockies between 1991 and 1995.

Christians face similar challenges spiritually. In his letter to the people of Colosse, Paul said he rejoiced to see their steadfastness in Christ despite others' attempts to take them captive with another way of thinking, one that would rob them of the peace of Christ (see Colossians 2:5–8). In verse 7, he described what kind of believer remains steadfast and is not taken captive: one who is *grounded, growing,* and *grateful.*

Grounded (*rooted*) By faith, you have been rooted in Christ, drawing from Him all that you need. How firm are your roots? Are you sinking roots in anything besides Christ?

Growing (*built up*) You have been placed on a solid foundation if you have trusted Christ to save you. Now keep building upon this. How? Paul said, "As you were taught." Epaphras

(Colossians 1:7) had taught the Colossians. They had learned the grace of God in truth. How's your construction going?

Grateful (*overflowing with thankfulness*) Paul taught that thankfulness is an attitude that protects the believer from losing peace and joy amid persecution or from being led astray by false teaching (See Philippians 4:4–7). Where's the level of your thankfulness?

Being spiritually steadfast isn't something that just happens. It takes work, and it is a process. Be determined and disciplined to be firmly grounded, always growing, and increasingly grateful.

—Bryan Hickerson

FOLLOW THROUGH

Of the three G's mentioned, which is the one that causes you the most difficulty? Do one thing today to help your grounding, something to help your growing, and one thing to help your gratefulness.

From the Playbook: Read Colossians 2.

NO. 49 CARLOS BAERGA The Cleveland Indians loved Carlos Baerga—the fact that he could get them 200 hits in a season and bat over .300. But Baerga got drawn into the lifestyle of a major leaguer, and he nearly threw it all away. But when Julio Franco helped him rededicate himself to Jesus, he returned to his former self on the field. "When you put everything in God's hands, He gives you life." Baerga retired with more than 1,500 hits and a .291 batting average.

50. FREE-TIME DANGER

"Let us throw off everything that hinders and the sin that so easily entangles."

HEBREWS 12:1

Longtime major league All-Star first baseman Mike Sweeney was always cautious about how he spent his free time when on the road for away games. He chose to go out with his teammates only when he thought the setting would be free of temptations that could possibly cause him to compromise his Christian values and personal witness.

FAST FACT:

Mike Sweeney finished his 13 years in Kansas City as the team's second all-time leading home-run hitter with 197.

It was not always easy for Sweeney to say "no" to various activities, but he wanted to put God, his wife, his family, and his career ahead of temporary pleasures that could possibly hurt the things and people he cares most about.

Hebrews 12:1 says, "Therefore, since we are surrounded by such a great a cloud of witnesses, let us throw off everything that hinders and the sin that so easily entangles, and let us run with perseverance the race marked out for us."

It is vital that we make a series of good choices throughout "the race" of life that Hebrews talks about. For starters, we can avoid harming others and ourselves by fleeing from temptations. Also, if we know that friends are going to participate in activities we don't agree with, we simply tell them we're not going.

Think about how your choices in those moments might adversely affect you tomorrow. And most important, consider whether or not your actions are pleasing to God.

When you're tempted to make a bad decision, think of athletes you've heard of who by one bad choice, such as taking drugs or gambling, destroyed their careers and reputation. Be on guard to protect what you've worked hard for and—most important—protect your Christian testimony.

—ROXANNE ROBBINS

FOLLOW THROUGH

Is there an activity in your life that is harming your Christian witness? If so, ask a close friend to hold you accountable for refraining from that activity.

From the Playbook: Read Matthew 7:13–29.

NO. 50 MIKE SWEENEY Injuries stopped Sweeney from reaching superstar status. While he had three seasons of more than 140 games played, he had several in which he missed a quarter of the season. Still he finished with a career average near .300 and with nearly 200 home runs—all because of the right attitude. "I want fans to see me on the last game of the season going 100 percent, and when they look at me, say, 'That's what being a Christian is all about.' "

51. NEVER GROW UP?

"The greatest among you should be like the youngest."
LUKE 22:26

It is absolutely amazing to me how quickly I forget. Not just forget where I put my cell phone or car keys but forget what life was like. I am not that far removed from rookie status as a major leaguer, and already I've forgotten how it felt to be a first-year player.

As a rookie, I was very coachable. I listened to everyone (possibly too many people) when told what I was doing wrong with my swing. I was humble. When the veterans wanted to dress me in a skirt or in a giant Batman costume, I was more than willing to do so. After all, I was new here, and I didn't want to upset those who knew more than I did.

FAST FACT:

Matt Diaz was a rookie for three years (2003-2005). He was called up and sent down five times in those three years. In 2006, he played in 124 games and hit .327.

Like I said, it's amazing how soon I forget, not just in baseball but also in life. When God blessed my wife, Leslee, and me with our first child, Nathan, I truly learned what Jesus was teaching His disciples when He said, "The greatest among you should be like the youngest." I saw my infant son and learned again what it means to trust—he had no hope of feeding himself. I learned humility—without Leslee and me, our son would lie in an unchanged diaper all day. Even as an infant, my son listened for his daddy's voice and turned toward it.

These are the new goals of my walk with Christ, and I hope you join me in pursuing them: We need to trust God, because we can't truly provide for ourselves. We need to be humble and open to having God "change" us. Most important, we need to listen for our heavenly "Daddy's" voice, look for it in the Bible, and do what He tells us.

Let's never grow out of doing this.

—MATT DIAZ

FOLLOW THROUGH

What are a couple of spiritual habits you have "outgrown"? Who are some children or younger people in your life you can watch and learn from?

From the Playbook: Read Mark 9:33–37 and then Mark 10:13–16 to see how Jesus used children as object lessons for His disciples.

NO. 51 TRAVIS FRYMAN Thanks to a teammate's wife, Fryman's life was transformed. When Travis played for Detroit, Frank Tanana's wife, Cathy, led Kathleen Fryman (Travis' wife) to faith in Christ. When Travis saw the change in her, he rededicated his life. Fryman was an All-Star third basemen for the Tigers and then Cleveland from 1990 through 2002, finishing with 1,776 hits and 223 home runs.

52. NO SAVES TODAY

"Our God is a God who saves; from the Sovereign Lord comes escape from death."

PSALM 68:20

On July 16, 2006, for the first time in 28 major league baseball seasons, a full schedule of games was played without a single save being recorded. Now, this kind of statistic can make you think one of two baseball-related thoughts right away.

First, it could make you think that perhaps there was something wrong with the state of relief pitchers that in all of the games played on July 16, 2006, not one relief pitcher could hold a lead (there were six blown saves). Or it could make you think, "Who on earth has the job of keeping track of these kinds of statistics, and why can't he find real work?"

FAST FACT:

The most saves ever recorded in a season was 62 by Francisco Rodriguez of the Angels in 2008.

Let's go another direction. Let's think about a very different kind of save. Imagine if a day were to go by in which there were no spiritual saves— if not one human on the face of the earth trusted Jesus Christ as Savior on a particular day. Of course, we don't know that this could ever happen, but just thinking about it might remind us that we have some work to do.

Many churches have a symbolic item at the front of the sanctuary that lets the church-goers know if someone trusted Jesus Christ—was saved—through the ministry of the church throughout the previous week. Let's say it is a candle that is lit to indicate that someone has been born again that week.

Seeing that candle encourages everyone in attendance. But arriving to see no candle lit can be seen as a challenge.

If it were up to us, would there be any candles lit? Would there be any saves today?

—DAVE BRANON

FOLLOW THROUGH

Is there someone close to you who respects you and may just be waiting for a word from you about finding peace with God? Think of a way to present the salvation found in Christ to him or her.

From the Playbook: Read Acts 1:1–8.

NO. 52 SAL BANDO A four-time All-Star, Bando was a leader of the Oakland A's during their heyday in the 1970s. It was during that time that Bando became a Christian, with the help of his manager Alvin Dark. Bando had 2,019 hits and 242 home runs in his 16-year career.

53. CONFESSIONS OF A SPORTS ADDICT

"You shall have no other gods before me."

DEUTERONOMY 5:7

We pulled into the parking lot in a do-or-die situation. The game was blaring on the radio. With the contest now in the 12th inning, the premise was clear. Win, and claim the divisional crown. Lose, and finish second. What to do?

I love our church's Sunday evening service. It's a terrific atmosphere of community and worship. But it had been 19 years since the team I so closely identify with had come remotely close to a sniff of the postseason. Surely I could linger in the van for a few moments longer.

My kids scrambled to catch up with friends. My wife struggled to extract the baby from the baby seat. I struggled with my emotions.

And I got out of the van.

"You shall have no other gods before me," God declares in His Rule Book (Deuteronomy 5:7). And so I prayed: "Help me, Lord, to put this in the proper perspective. You know how passionate I am about baseball. Help me put it aside and worship You in the next few moments."

Inside the church, I watched the praise band warming up. The worship leader's 2-year-old son gleefully tossed drum-

FAST FACT:

The Tampa Bay Rays were the last franchise to make the postseason playoffs, which they finally did in 2008. The Washington Nationals (Montreal Expos) have not played October baseball since 1981.

sticks off the platform and chased them. My own toddler clung to me as he watched the band in fascination. Ah, yes. Things were as they should be.

After church (a great service, by the way), a hearing-impaired friend who shared my zeal for baseball approached. He signed his disgust emphatically. "The bad guys beat us! We stink."

I took the loss philosophically. Wait till next year. Tonight at least, I had my priorities in order.

—TIM GUSTAFSON

FOLLOW THROUGH

Do you routinely give up spiritual things for less important matters? How much time each day do you give to reading God's Word and praying? What changes do you need to make in your priorities?

From the Playbook: Read Psalm 100.

NO. 53 LANCE PARRISH Parrish was part of something special in 1984 when his Detroit Tigers won 35 of their first 40 games and went on to win the World Series. Parrish hit 33 home runs that year—ending his career with 324 long blasts. Of his faith, Parrish said, "The Bible teaches us values and principles and to put our faith in Christ."

54. RECEIVE AND BELIEVE

"He gave the right to become children of God."

JOHN 1:12

Growing up in Georgia, major league outfielder J. D. Drew knew plenty of Bible stories. He went to church regularly. But it wasn't until high school that the future National League All-Star became a child of God.

As a youngster, J. D. knew about God. He knew about Jesus Christ. And he even had a basic understanding of the Holy Spirit. J. D. Drew knew *about* the Trinity.

But it wasn't until he was 16 years old that J. D. took the words of John 1:12 to heart: "Yet to all who received him, to those who believed in his name, he gave the right to become children of God."

It wasn't until J. D. truly *believed* in the person and work of Jesus Christ, and *received* Christ's sacrifice on the cross as payment for his sin that he became a child of God.

Are you a part of God's eternal family? If you're not sure, ask yourself these questions: Do I have knowledge *about* God, or do I have a relationship *with* Him? Have I ever placed my faith (belief) in Jesus Christ and received Christ and His sacrificial death as payment for my sin?

If you answered "no" but would like to be adopted into God's eternal family, you can be right now! Pray to God using the words of the following prayer.

FAST FACT:
J. D. and his brothers Tim and Stephen were all first-round draft picks by major league teams. They are the only three brothers to have that designation.

"God, I confess that I am a sinner. I repent of my sin, and place my faith in Your Son, Jesus Christ. I believe that Jesus sacrificed His perfect life to cleanse me of my sin. I receive Jesus Christ as my Lord and Savior. I receive Your gift of eternal life and a place in Your eternal family. Amen."

—ROB BENTZ

FOLLOW THROUGH

If you prayed this prayer of salvation—welcome to the family! The journey you are now embarking on is filled with many great times and also some challenging times. You can strengthen your new faith by talking with God in prayer, reading the Bible, and spending time with other Christians. Please write to us and tell us about your decision, using the address in the back of this book.

From the Playbook: Read John 1.

NO. 54 J. D. DREW During his junior year of college, Drew was the best player in the nation. That led to his being the second player picked in the 1997 draft. Injuries during his career stopped him from becoming a superstar, but he had some big highlights, including hitting a grand slam in the 2007 playoffs, winning the World Series with Boston, and playing in the All-Star Game. A Christian since he was 16, Drew says, "The plan of salvation is so simple, but so many people miss it because they think they can work their way to heaven."

55. KEEP YOUR EYES ON THE PRIZE

"I press on toward the goal to win the prize for which God has called me heavenward in Christ Jesus."

PHILIPPIANS 3:14

Although he was an All-Star five times, captured the American League MVP Award twice, and holds numerous Chicago White Sox records, Frank Thomas was still missing something he greatly desired. Through all his individual accomplishments, Thomas kept his eye on the prize of a World Series championship.

FAST FACT:
Frank Thomas, a career .300-plus hitter and in the Top 20 of all time in home runs, won back-to-back AL MVP honors in 1993 and 1994.

Over the first 15 years of his career, he had to endure teams that were not competitive or were underachievers. He persevered through criticism from the media and the organization. In the late summer of 2005, he had to struggle through an ankle injury that limited his playing time to one month during his team's championship race. But in October 2005, when the Chicago White Sox won the World Series, Thomas was finally rewarded with the prize he longed for. If asked, I'm confident Thomas would say that all the sweat, pain, and difficulties were well worth it in the end.

As followers of Jesus, we also have a prize we need to keep our eye on. We must focus on the eternal "prize" for which we strive. Our prize is Jesus Christ himself! Out of our love relationship with Him, we persevere through trials, temptations, and when necessary, persecutions for His name's sake. There is no greater calling in life, and there is no greater prize. The author of Hebrews 12:1, 2 encourages us by saying, "Let us run with perseverance the race marked out for us. Let us fix our eyes on Jesus, the author and perfecter of our faith."

One day each of us will stand before our Lord Jesus. On that day, our desire should be to hear the words, "Well done, good and faithful servant!" (Matthew 25:23). When we see the prize—when we see Jesus and hear those words from His lips—we will know that everything we had to endure was well worth it.

—MICKEY WESTON

FOLLOW THROUGH

What tends to distract you into taking your eyes off Jesus? What is one thing you can do today to help you "fix" your mind, will, and emotions on Jesus and His purposes for your life?

From the Playbook: Meditate on Hebrews 12:1–3.

NO. 55 GARY GAETTI Gary Gaetti's story is a bit unusual, although Scripture would suggest otherwise. When he became a Christian while playing for the Minnesota Twins, he faced fierce persecution from teammates and others for changing his lifestyle (I Peter 4:12–16). Yet he never backed down, simply saying, "When the Lord saved me, He took away the desire to party." When he retired in 2000, he had hit 360 home runs and had accumulated 2,280 hits, plus a World Series ring.

56. WHO IS STEERING?

*"In his heart a man plans his course,
but the Lord determines his steps."*

PROVERBS 16:9

We all have bad days, bumps in the road, valleys, trials—however you want to categorize it. Life is confusing, and sometimes it downright stinks.

As baseball players, we have to learn to deal with things when they don't go our way. You see, for a hitter in baseball, if he fails 70 percent of the time he's an All-Star. For a pitcher, giving up a hit, throwing a ball instead of a strike, giving up a key run—these all spell failure. Baseball success isn't based on who succeeds more but on who fails less. It has been correctly called a game of failure.

How do I view life in an atmosphere where failure seems to loom in every corner? Like a tandem bicycle! You see, a tandem bicycle has two seats, two sets of pedals, and obviously has two people riding it. But it has only one person steering. Because I have accepted Jesus as my Savior, whenever I get into tough times, I remind myself that on my tandem bicycle He is my other rider. Since only one rider can steer, I have to always ask myself if Jesus is steering the bike and if I am on the back pedaling and working as hard as I possibly can.

FAST FACT:
In the 2007 World Series, Jeremy pitched three innings with an ERA of 0.00.

If Jesus is guiding my steps and steering the bike, than all I have to do is pedal and work hard. If I do that, than I will end up being exactly where God wants me to be!

—JEREMY AFFELDT

FOLLOW THROUGH

In what you do in life, where does failure loom? How does it help you to know that Jesus is steering and that you can ask Him to help you through the tough times?

From the Playbook: Read Psalm 30:1–3.

NO. 56 TERRY PENDLETON Pendleton was not a .300 hitter. Well, except for 1991 when he led the NL in hitting with a .319 mark. The next year he had 199 hits and a .311 average. In no other full season did he hit .300 or better. Yet he ended his 15-year career with 1,897 hits and a respectable .270 average—and a waiting career as a successful hitting coach. How does he make decisions? "I stop and think how Christ would want me to handle the situation."

57. WHERE HAVE YOU GONE, JOE DIMAGGIO?

"For all have sinned and fall short of the glory of God."
ROMANS 3:23

Several years ago Pulitzer Prize-winning author Richard Ben Cramer came out with a book called *Joe DiMaggio: The Hero's Life.* The biography about the baseball legend became a *New York Times* bestseller and was described by Larry King as "an extraordinary biography."

The book's endorsements that struck me the most, however, were by Ken Garcia of the *San Francisco Chronicle* and Daniel Okrent of *Time* magazine. Garcia's review said, "An often brilliant and deeply disturbing look into the rise of one of the country's modern-day giants." Okrent added, "DiMaggio is rendered so vividly you almost want to look away."

FAST FACT:

The most astounding record in baseball, some suggest, is DiMaggio's 56-game hitting streak in 1941.

What could be "disturbing" about the life of this rich and famous athlete? What could make someone want to "look away" from DiMaggio, the key to the New York Yankees' dominance in the 30s through 50s and the larger-than-life sports hero who managed to land movie star Marilyn Monroe as his wife?

The answer is that stardom wasn't the only companion in DiMaggio's life. He was also accompanied by emptiness and pain, as we all are. The Bible clearly states that there's not a person on this earth, regardless of worldly fame, whose life is free of a dark side. "For all have sinned and fall short of the glory of God" (Romans 3:23). We've all done things we wouldn't want revealed in a biography of our lives. All of this could make life seem like a bum deal—except for this: Our story becomes beautiful through and through when we reflect on the truth that in Christ we have been redeemed. He alone brightens our life and makes it truly worth living.

—ROXANNE ROBBINS

FOLLOW THROUGH

Read a biography of a person whose life was changed by Jesus Christ. Notice how redemption provides light for life.

From the Playbook: Read Romans 3.

57. ALVIN DARK Known mostly as a great manager, especially with the Oakland A's of the 70s, Dark was also an outstanding player. A career .289 hitter, he pounded out 2,089 hits in a 14-year career. He led the NL in doubles in 1951 with 41. As a manager, he won 994 games and one World Series. His name was Dark, but his humor was light: "The Lord taught me to love everybody, but the last ones I learned to love were the sportswriters."

58. ZOOM-ZOOM

*"Be all the more eager to make your calling
and election sure."*

2 PETER 1:10

When Joel Zumaya broke into the majors in 2006, he had the fastest fastball in baseball. As a rookie with Detroit, the hard-throwing right-hander was officially clocked at 103 mph on a pitch thrown in Oakland. Unofficial radar-gun readings of 104 mph have added to Zumaya's *en fuego*-fastball reputation.

Zumaya is sometimes known as "Zum-zum" (Zoom-zoom) because of the smoke he throws. In 2006, the 21-year-old impressed MLB teams around the league with his ability to fire pitches fast and accurately. In 62 games that season, "Zum-zum" had 97 strikeouts and just 42 walks.

FAST FACT:

Mark Wohlers (Atlanta 1995) was the first pitcher to reach 103 mph.

Will he ever top the 103.0 mph mark he set in 2006? Only time will tell, but each pitch packs excitement when Joel Zumaya is on the mound.

I think God would like all believers to share a characteristic with "Zum-zum." No, I don't mean that all of us should be firing fastballs! Instead God wants us to be "fast" and accurate in how we grow our faith in Him. He wants us to be *eager* to grow in character, while *accurate* in the Christlike traits we pursue.

The apostle Peter wrote, "Make every effort to add to your faith goodness ... knowledge ... self-control ... perseverance ... godliness ... brotherly kindness ... love" (2 Peter

1:5–7). When we display these traits, we're showing that we are true believers in Jesus.

Be eager and accurate today in the godly qualities you are striving to attain!

—TOM FELTEN

FOLLOW THROUGH

Carefully read over the list of character qualities listed in 2 Peter 1:5–7. Which one should you be pursuing today? Pray to God and ask Him to help you develop this trait in your life.

From the Playbook: Read 2 Peter 1:2–11.

NO. 58 MIKE TIMLIN Sometimes athletes are recognized more for perseverance than for blazing talent. Mike Timlin is one of those. Beginning in 1991, he just showed up and did whatever he could to help his team—appearing in more than one thousand games as a relief pitcher, including 81 in 2005. Those 1,000-plus games put him in the Top 10 all-time in appearances by a pitcher. Says Timlin of his faith, "God works in my life every day." A bit like Mike Timlin on the field, who seemed to work almost every day.

59. YOU'VE ALWAYS GOT HOPE

"[God] has given us new birth into a living hope through the resurrection of Jesus Christ from the dead."

1 Peter 1:3

On December 24, 2004, the sports world lost one of its truly good guys. Johnny Oates, who had managed both the Baltimore Orioles and Texas Rangers, died after a 3-year battle with a brain tumor. Not long before he died, Johnny spoke with his good friend Chuck Swirsky on Sports Spectrum Radio.

"Through my illness, I've learned not as much of what I am, but I learned what I was. I have found out that my desire and my hunger is to know more about God, to be more like Him. I thought I was walking that way, but now that I get into the Bible and read it, that's the reason they call it the Living Word. It really speaks to me now. It's saying be patient, that I've got a plan for you. It's not to harm you, not to hurt you, but it's to give you hope.

"That word has come out to me so many times. Hope. The hope of glory. Hope in eternity through my salvation. I've been promised through the Word that my hope is eternity. My hope for everyone is that they come to have a personal relationship with our Lord. If you have that relationship—if you've accepted Him as your Lord and Savior, you get that same promise.

FAST FACT:
Johnny Oates managed 1,544 games in his major league career, winning 797 and losing 746.

"I know our God is awesome, and I know He is interested in me. Every once in a while, I feel like I'm at the end of my rope, but the bottom line is that I'm never near the end of my rope. Once saved, you've always got hope."

Today, Johnny Oates is enjoying the fruits of his faith—the glorious realization of his hope in Jesus Christ. Can you echo his words?
—Sports Spectrum Radio

FOLLOW THROUGH

Are you facing a circumstance that seems to be devoid of hope? What is something Johnny Oates said that can give you courage in the face of hopelessness?

From the Playbook: Read Psalm 25.

NO. 59 JAY BELL Bespectacled Jay Bell was not afraid to give himself up for his team. In both 1990 and 1991, for example, Bell led the league in sacrifice hits for Pittsburgh. The two-time All-Star spent 18 seasons in the majors, finishing with 1,963 hits. He recognized the difficulty of being a strong believer in the secular world: "Being a Christian is a challenge on a daily basis, whether you're in baseball or in any other walk of life."

60. WHEN THINGS DON'T GO YOUR WAY

"He must increase, but I must decrease."
JOHN 3:30 (NAS)

All of us who desire to be successful in this world face a huge struggle. We often seek things that have little eternal worth. I have found myself conforming to this world in order to achieve goals that, when I look back on them, aren't worth much.

When I step onto a major league baseball field to play a game, it is easy to forget that what is most important to me is my relationship with God. Dealing with failure is a common occurrence in baseball, and sometimes it can be painful. It is at these times that I must turn to the Lord.

FAST FACT:
Michael Barrett hit .287 with 16 home runs and 65 RBI in 2004.

I have tried through the years to be a quality role model and to set a good example, but there are times when I give in to the pressure. I have found myself asking for forgiveness for a few poorly chosen words or actions. I know that a person does not have to be a baseball player to have these feelings or thoughts—but our missteps are magnified for all to see. I have found that the best way to be successful is to think as the apostle John suggested, "[Christ] must increase, but I must decrease" (John 3:30).

Through my relationship with Jesus, I have learned to deal with these struggles better. Because I have a perfect God who loves me in spite of all my imperfections, it is easier to rely less on the people around me for the love, support, and care that I need—and more on Him.

That is what allows me to rest easier at night when things are not going my way.

—MICHAEL BARRETT

FOLLOW THROUGH

What hasn't gone your way in the past few days? Maybe you didn't strike out or have a passed ball, but you probably failed in a way important to you. Were you able to allow Christ to increase and yourself to decrease in that incident—trusting a perfect God to sort it all out?

From the Playbook: Read Romans 8:28–39.

NO. 60 HOWARD JOHNSON Jokes about having the same name as a hotel chain aside, HoJo did pretty well for himself in the majors. During one five-year span, he hit 157 home runs for the New York Mets—ending his career in 1995 with 228 round-trip blasts. Not bad for a guy who stands just 5′10″ tall. But he knew what he stood for. "We're supposed to stand for consistency and all the good that's in the world through Jesus."

61. TRASH TALK, VINTAGE 1925

"Do not answer a fool according to his folly."
PROVERBS 26:4

"Answer a fool according to his folly."
PROVERBS 26:5

Many fans bemoan the escalation of trash talk in sports. But it's nothing new.

In 1925, future Hall of Fame catcher Mickey Cochrane was a rookie with the Philadelphia Athletics, a team full of swagger and potential. The A's quickly surged to a 5 ½ game lead in the American League.

FAST FACT:
Cochrane, a .320 hitter, had his career curtailed by a beaning in 1937.

Despite manager Connie Mack's warnings, the Athletics couldn't resist taunting Ty Cobb when they beat his Detroit Tigers. Furious, Cobb vowed to knock the A's out of the pennant race.

Less than a week later, the Athletics stumbled back to Detroit on a three-game losing streak. As Cochrane recalls it, Cobb "went wild," going 12 for 16, stealing "everything but home plate," and snagging every ball hit his way. Cobb's actions subdued Philadelphia's mere words, and they skidded into a 13-game slide.

When an oversized warrior named Goliath towered over the Israelite army, he stooped to a little trash talk (1 Samuel 17:8–10). But a shepherd boy named David silenced the garrulous giant with a sling and a stone. Before hurling his projectile, David called Goliath out: "You come against me with sword and spear and javelin, but I come against you in the name of the Lord Almighty" (v. 45).

Two proverbs seem to contradict each other. Proverbs 26:4 says, "Do not answer a fool according to his folly, or you will be like him yourself." But verse 5 instructs us: "Answer a fool according to his folly, or he will be wise in his own eyes."

Trash talk springs out of foolish arrogance, which leads inevitably to a fall. By relying on God, David knew precisely how and when to respond.

—TIM GUSTAFSON

FOLLOW THROUGH

Can trash talk honor God? What was different about David's response to Goliath in 1 Samuel 17:45? How might Proverbs 15:1-2 apply to trash talk? Do you let trash talk bother you? Read Proverbs 26:2 for help.

From the Playbook: Read 1 Samuel 17:45–50.

NO. 61 ANDY VAN SLYKE Van Slyke led the league in hits once, in doubles once, and in triples once, but it was his fielding that was worth the price of admission. He won five Gold Gloves for his prowess in the outfield. A three-time All-Star, Van Slyke trusted Christ through Baseball Chapel. He made a key observation about Christians and athletes: "We need to give guys some time to grow [spiritually] before we ask them to be God's spokesmen."

62. LOVE AND BASEBALL

This is how God showed his love among us: He sent his one and only Son into the world . . . as an atoning sacrifice."

1 JOHN 4:9–10

Finally, his boyhood dream was coming true. After four years of earning his way through the minors, Tim Burke was given a chance to play in the big leagues in 1985. After making it to the majors with the Montreal Expos, Burke quickly proved that he was good enough to be there by setting the record for the most relief appearances (78) by a rookie pitcher. Several years later, he would sign a $600,000 contract with the Cincinnati Reds. However, three months after signing, Burke retired.

FAST FACT:

Burke was 26 years old when he broke into the big leagues with Montreal (now Washington) on April 8, 1985.

Yes, that's right. You see, along the way Tim and his wife Christine had adopted four children with special needs—two daughters from South Korea, a son from Guatemala, and another son from Vietnam. All the children were born with serious illnesses or defects. After considering the grueling schedule of the major leagues, Tim decided he needed to retire at the age of 34 so he could help raise his children. He said at the time, "Baseball is going to be just fine without me. But I'm the only father my children have." Tim learned what love was really about—sacrifice.

"This is how God showed His love among us: He sent his one and only Son into the world that we might live through him" (1 John 4:9). God modeled what love is by sacrificing His Son for us on the cross. Sometimes, as Tim did, we are called to make sacrifices of our own. What in your life are you willing to sacrifice? Consider today how you can love others through your sacrifice.

—MOLLY RAMSEYER

FOLLOW THROUGH

Is someone around you in need? Sacrifice your agenda or your time to show love to that person today.

From the Playbook: Read 1 Corinthians 13 to see the characteristics of true love.

NO. 62 ANDRE THORNTON Tragedy marked the early career of Andre Thornton. He lost his wife and a daughter in a car accident. He endured through his grief to become a Cleveland hero. He banged out 253 home runs during a career that included two 100-plus RBI seasons. He retired in 1987 from baseball. "The Bible contains the instructions the Lord has given us to guide our lives," Thornton has said. And he still uses that instruction as a husband, father, and businessman.

63. GET IN THE BOX

"For God so loved the world that he gave
his one and only Son."

JOHN 3:16

John 3:16 never really hit home with me until I was twenty-two years old and playing minor league baseball.

I remember in college watching a pitcher dominate in the major leagues, and I brashly said, "I believe I could get a hit off him." My statement was tested two years later. That same pitcher was finishing a rehabilitation assignment with a minor league team, and he had one last start before he was to go back to the big leagues. That start was against our minor league team. I immediately began researching how he had done in his last rehab starts. I called friends on other minor league teams that had faced him. At the end of one of these talks, I again said, "I believe I can hit him."

Then the game came, and it was clear that this ace was feeling good. I was batting fifth, and he retired every batter he faced in the first inning. Our fourth batter stepped into the batter's box and BAM! The pitcher nailed him right in the back. By the sound of it, the pitcher had recovered his velocity. While the coach and trainer were checking on my teammate to make sure he was still all in one piece, the umpire asked me, "Think you can hit him?"

At this moment my belief was asked to act, and here is where my story meets John 3:16. Do I believe in Jesus because heaven sounds better than hell? Do I believe in Him in my

FAST FACT:
Matt Diaz played college baseball at Florida State before being drafted by Tampa Bay in 1999.

head because I've researched His existence? Or do I truly believe and reflect Him and His teachings in my actions? It's time for us Christians to daily get in the batter's box. Our belief needs to result in action.

To finish the story, I did get in the box against the Cy Young runner-up, and once I finished shaking, I hit a double. Amazing what a little belief that's put into action can do.

—MATT DIAZ

FOLLOW THROUGH

When is the last time your belief led to action? What is one thing you feel God calling you to change if you truly believe in His Son?

From the Playbook: Read James 2:14–25 and decide for yourself what James means when he says, "Even the demons believe that—and shudder."

NO. 63 JOSH HAMILTON Everything about Josh Hamilton's life surprises people. That he turned to drugs after being the No. 1 pick in the draft in 1999. That he turned to faith after drugs nearly killed him. That he returned to baseball to become one of its top sluggers.

With much of his career ahead of him, he established himself as a legend in 2008 by hitting 28 Home Run Derby blasts at Yankee Stadium. No one expected that.

Says Hamilton, "It's such a great thing to see how God never leaves your side."

64. THE VALUE OF SACRIFICE

"God presented him as a sacrifice of atonement, through faith in his blood."

ROMANS 3:25

Any good middle infielder in the major leagues knows that to cover the middle of the diamond, he's got to make physical sacrifices. The game's best shortstops and second basemen will at some point during a season have to sacrifice their bodies to make diving, run-saving plays on less-than-forgiving artificial turf.

FAST FACT:

Placido Polanco played the entire 2007 season at second base without making an error.

Some of today's stars—Orlando Cabrera, Omar Vizquel, Placido Polanco, Jimmy Rollins, and others—have turned self-sacrificing plays into the norm. They throw their bodies into the action with little or no thought. Their bodies take a beating for their all-out effort.

Thankfully, God does not require us to offer physical sacrifices to please and honor Him. We are not expected to sacrifice health and well-being for Him as a prerequisite for salvation.

God provided His Son, Jesus, as the ultimate sacrifice. The sacrificial blood that Jesus shed on the cross atones for the sins of those who believe. His sacrifice makes the relationship with the Father possible. Only through Christ's sacrificial death on the cross is the gap between our sin and God's holiness covered. Jesus' sacrifice bridges that tremendous gap. His sacrifice is the only act that sets believers free—free from a life of vainly striving to atone for our sin. Free from an eternity apart from God!

Self-sacrificial activity is still required of a good middle infielder, but it is not needed for the forgiveness of your sin and mine—Jesus took care of that.

—ROB BENTZ

FOLLOW THROUGH

Take a few moments to meditate on the significance of the sacrificial atonement that God provided for you in His Son, Jesus. Through prayer, tell the Father how grateful you are.

From the Playbook: Read Romans 3:21–31.

NO. 64 BOBBY RICHARDSON One of the classiest Christian baseball players ever, Richardson was the MVP of the 1960 World Series when he had a record 12 RBI. One of the grandest moments of his life was when Mickey Mantle shared with Richardson that he had trusted Jesus as Savior—just five days before Mantle died in August 1995. Richardson coached at Liberty and South Carolina after he stopped playing. "The Lord has been really good. There have been tough times, but the Lord is faithful."

65. THE POWER OF PRAYER

*"Since the day we heard about you, we have
not stopped praying for you."*

COLOSSIANS 1:9

Drafted by the former Milwaukee Braves at age 18, Ed Herrmann was excited to follow in the footsteps of his grandfather, who had pitched in the major leagues in 1918. Herrmann went on to spend more than a decade in the big leagues, earning All-Star honors along the way.

On his Web site, www.edherrmann.com, Hermann reflects on that era of his life saying, "I had what I thought was a fulfilling life, but on December 23, 1991, my life changed forever. That is the day my father passed away. For many years my mother and brother were active Christians and my father and I weren't. I know now that we both were the recipients of many prayers.

FAST FACT:

*In 1970,
Ed Herrmann
hit 19 home
runs for the
Chicago
White Sox.*

"Although I thought there was a God, I never knew how to reach Him. I also thought I had everything I ever needed . . . fame, baseball, money, and a lot of bad habits. The fateful day in 1991 . . . the day I felt so lonely and lost was the first time I knelt down to pray to Jesus to ask for help and invite Him into my life. Since that day, I know I have sinned, but because I have the Lord Jesus Christ I know I am forgiven and I will have eternal life. Now I know I have everything I ever needed, and each day continues to bring new blessings."

Just as Herrmann's mother and brother prayed for him many years, commit to praying diligently for the people God places in your life. Ask the Holy Spirit to help them know the full love of Christ.

—ROXANNE ROBBINS

FOLLOW THROUGH

Pray for a friend or family member, that he or she will experience God in a deeper way.

From the Playbook: Read Colossians 1:1–9.

NO. 65 TROT NIXON In 2004, Trot Nixon rode the Boston express to their surprising and historic World Series win. He hit .357 in that series to help the Sox beat the St. Louis Cardinals. His career had its ups and downs with injuries, but he could handle it, saying, "We can persevere, through good times or bad, because we're not alone. Jesus went through it too. He will never leave us."

66. HALL OF FAME STAIN

"You were washed, you were sanctified, you were justified, in the name of the Lord Jesus Christ."

1 CORINTHIANS 6:11

In an attempt to fool players and spectators in Des Moines, Iowa, Cap Anson dyed his hair and stained his skin. Apparently, he didn't want anyone to recognize him when he played for the rival Clinton ballclub.

If Cap's subterfuge seems odd, consider that the era was the late 1860s, and he was to be paid the princely sum of $50 to play a single game. Unfortunately, on his way to the game Cap bumped into his father at the train depot. The elder Anson wasn't fooled in the least, and he sent Cap home. It took days for the stain to wear off. Worst of all, he didn't collect the $50.

Ironically, Cap became one of the main reasons the major leagues once excluded African-Americans. Cap Anson was a Hall of Fame player, but his record is marred with the stain of racism.

We can all be taunted by our past errors. We all have regrets, locked tightly away where we hope no one can see them. We can cover up the stain, but time won't eradicate it.

The apostle Paul listed a long litany of heinous sins when writing to the struggling church in Corinth. Then he reminded

FAST FACT:
Cap Anson was the first player to collect 3,000 hits, the first manager to hold spring training, and the first to call for a hit-and-run.

them: "That is what some of you were. But you were washed, you were sanctified, you were justified in the name of the Lord Jesus Christ and by the Spirit of our God" (1 Corinthians 6:11).

Perhaps you are living with the burden of guilt. Have you ever considered allowing God to relieve you of that guilt? He wants to do it. Our sins are precisely why Jesus went to the cross. He offers forgiveness and a chance to begin anew.

—Tim Gustafson

FOLLOW THROUGH

Have you ever confessed your sins and regrets to Jesus? What does God promise to do if you confess your sins? (1 John 1:9).

From the Playbook: Read 1 John 1:5–10.

NO. 66 MANNY SANGUILLEN Manny laid down his glove and picked up a fork when his playing days were over in Pittsburgh. He went from catching for the Pirates to cooking BBQ for Pirates fans outside the ballpark. While the backstop for the Buccos, he was cooking: More than 1,500 hits, batted .375 in two World Series, made the All-Star team. "My faith is in the Lord," says Manny. "I know that Jesus came and died for us."

67. WHAT IF THERE'S MORE?

Strike Zone:
Grappling with change

"God had planned something better for us."
HEBREWS 11:40

Did you know that Babe Ruth started his major league career as a pitcher? That's right. In his first six seasons, the man who eventually became legendary for hitting 714 home runs was an ace southpaw.

From 1915–18, Ruth won 78 games for the Red Sox, more than any other left-handed pitcher in the majors. He also holds the record for the longest complete game win in World Series history. In 1916, he pitched 14 innings in a Boston victory over the Brooklyn Dodgers in the Fall Classic.

FAST FACT:
Babe Ruth is the only player to hit three home runs twice in a World Series game (1926 and 1928).

While Ruth was a highly successful pitcher, he didn't turn into a major home run threat until he made the change from pitcher to outfield. In fact, Ruth hit only 27 home runs in five seasons before he became a regular outfielder in 1919. In 1920, his first year with the New York Yankees, he swatted an unheard of 54 home runs.

A major change can be unsettling. It can force us out of our comfort zone and into the unknown. Still, a change is often the very thing we need to become more of who we are truly meant to be.

That's what happened to Moses. Although he was orphaned as a baby, he eventually became a member of Egypt's royal household (Exodus 2:10). Life seemed to be going well, but

God had other plans. Changes were on the horizon that would eventually shape him into a powerful leader who would lead God's people out of slavery and on to the Promised Land (Deuteronomy 34:10–12).

Sometimes God calls us to make a significant change, even when life appears to be going well, because He has something more in mind. Are you ready and willing for the change?

—JEFF OLSON

FOLLOW THROUGH

Ask God how He might be using the changes in your life to lead you to something more. If change scares you, ask God for the courage to proceed.

From the Playbook: Read the stories of change in Hebrews 11.

NO. 67 JEFF FRANCOEUR He burst on the scene in 2005 for the Atlanta Braves, hitting 14 home runs and hitting .300 in just 70 games. In 2006 and 2007, he showed at age 22 and 23 how good he could be with 48 home runs and 208 RBI in those two seasons. Whether he continues to have a long, productive career, he had one of the coolest quotes ever when asked in 2007 about his goals: "To lead two people to the Lord," he said.

68. CONSPIRACY THEORY

Strike Zone:
Knowing when to get involved

"Mordecai found out about the plot."

ESTHER 2:22

As conspiracies go, it wasn't all that exciting. But it made for some big changes in baseball back in the 1980s.

Owners had grown tired of paying large salaries for baseball players, so they got together and conspired to change things. They decided that they would not sign any of the major free agents on the market.

Big problem. Once the Players Association found out about this, they couldn't get their lawyers on the phone fast enough. Lawsuits followed, and this plan, named *collusion*, has not happened again.

At least the baseball owners didn't get hanged like two officials in the Esther conspiracy story.

Unfortunately for them and fortunately for the king, Mordecai discovered their plan. Through Esther, Mordecai got word to the king about the plot. You can imagine that Xerxes was exasperated. Soon the two conspirators were hanging out for all to see.

This conspiracy was a tiny incident in the king's life, but it was significant because it showed the growing respect the king had for Mordecai.

Later, when Haman was about ready to carry out a plan to have Mordecai killed, God would cause the story of Mordecai's heroic deed to be re-read to him. When he was reminded

FAST FACT:
Kirk Gibson, hero of the 1988 World Series for the Los Angeles Dodgers, was one victim of collusion.

of what Mordecai had done for him, Haman's plans were reversed, and Haman, not Mordecai, got the gallows.

What should we do when we see wrongdoing? Get involved or let it slide? Mordecai did the courageous thing. He reported the conspiracy plan, saved the king's life, and preserved his own.

"Lord, give us the courage to react properly when we see wrongdoing."

—DAVE BRANON

FOLLOW THROUGH

Are you aware of someone's plans to do wrong? What should you do? Be wise, but careful with that information.

From the Playbook: Read Esther 2.

NO. 68 REGGIE SANDERS For a while there, it seemed that every time you turned around, Sanders was in the World Series with a new team: 2001, D-Backs; 2002, Giants; 2004, Cards. Not known as a home run hitter, he still managed to park 305 blasts in his distinguished, 17-season career. "I played for eight major league teams. I may not understand the purpose I've moved around so many times, but the Lord has a purpose for this."

69. TOOLS OF THE TRADE

"Set an example for the believers in speech, in life, in love, in faith and in purity."

1 TIMOTHY 4:12

Each of the 30 major league baseball teams employs scouts who scour the United States, Latin America, and other regions of the world in search of that "special" player—the one referred to as the "5-tool" player. The 5-tool guy runs like the wind, hits for power, hits for average, possesses a "cannon" for an arm, and plays great defense. The individual gifted with all of these tools is destined for greatness alongside the likes of perennial All-Stars Alex Rodriguez and Vladimir Guerrero. The baseball world stands in awe of the abilities of these high-quality players, and they are indeed rare.

FAST FACT:
Mickey Weston played for the Orioles, Blue Jays, Phillies, and Mets in his five-year major league career.

A high-quality example of a believer in Jesus Christ should not be as hard to find as a star athlete—but it often is. Jesus has called each of His followers to be a "5-tool" disciple. In 1 Timothy 4:12, the apostle Paul challenged Timothy, who was living in a culture much like ours, to stand out from the crowd and provide "an example for the believers."

To be a "5-tool" disciple, we must consider the way we speak, the conduct of our lives, and how we love others (especially other believers: John 13:35). Scripture also calls us to display trust in God under difficult circumstances and to maintain godly control over our minds and bodies. These are the tools that will distinguish believers in Jesus from the rest of the players on life's playing field.

We may not possess the tools to be a top All-Star on the baseball field, but each of us has the capability of pointing others to Jesus and bringing glory to God when we "set an example" as a "5-tool" disciple.

—MICKEY WESTON

FOLLOW THROUGH

Which tool (speech, life, love, faith, or purity) do you need to work on to become a better "example for the believers"? What will you do today to improve that area?

From the Playbook: Read Acts 4.

NO. 69 FELIPE ALOU Like Al Dark, Felipe Alou's successful managerial career overshadows a fine career on the field. A .286 hitter in 17 seasons, Alou had 2,054 wins as a manager and 2,101 hits as a player. In 1994, after he led Montreal to a strike-shortened record of 70-47, he said, "The Lord seemed to tell me, 'I didn't send you here to win the pennant; I sent you here to be a witness for me.'"

"Enter the Most Holy Place by the blood of Jesus."
HEBREWS 10:19

When you watch a big league baseball game on television, have you ever noticed how many times the network shows the team's general manager? Watch a New York Yankees game, and you're sure to see general manager Brian Cashman. Watch a Detroit Tigers game, and Dave Dombrowski will always get a few minutes of airtime. Former Atlanta Braves GM John Schuerholz was always good for a cameo during a Braves broadcast.

FAST FACT:
John Schuerholz was Atlanta's GM from 1990-2007.

It seems the reason the television producers show the general manager is the assumed intrigue we can observe in the impressions on the faces of the baseball architects of our favorite ballclub while they witness the on-field product they have created.

Did you ever wonder what God thinks of the product(s) He has created? Ever wonder if He is pleased or frustrated about His creation?

Throughout the Bible we read of both God's pleasure and His unhappiness with the people He created. For those who are followers of Christ, God has a special look: a look of favor. We are clean in God's eyes. Why?

In the New Testament book of Hebrews we find the reason. Christ-followers have confidence to enter the Most Holy Place—before the very throne of God—because of Jesus' sacrificial death on the cross. In Hebrews 10, the writer reminds us that we can "draw near to God with a sincere heart in full assurance of faith" (v. 22) because of "the blood of Jesus" (v. 19).

When God looks upon His creation and sees followers of Jesus like you and me, He sees us as clean because of the sacrificial blood of Christ. That's a great feeling!

—ROB BENTZ

FOLLOW THROUGH

Spend a few moments in prayer, thanking God for the favor that is yours because of Jesus and His sacrificial death on the cross. Begin to think of God looking at you with eyes of love, brought on by Jesus' sacrifice.

From the Playbook: Meditate on Hebrews 10:19–22.

NO. 70 KEVIN SEITZER The hits just kept coming for Seitzer in 1987. In his first full season in the majors, he led the league in hits with 207, and he finished sixth in the batting race at .323. Seitzer was never able to duplicate that season—but he ended up being a two-time All-Star with 1,557 career hits. He finished with a .295 batting average. Saved during his career, Seitzer says, "Jesus showed me that He's the One who takes away all those things that had been ruining my life."

71. NOTHING GREATER

Strike Zone:
Cherishing a relationship with God

"Present your bodies a living and holy sacrifice."
ROMANS 12:1 (NAS)

As Christians in this world, it is sometimes hard to continually stand for Christ. But what we must realize is that we cannot do it alone. We need support to make it through the good times and the bad.

The way I get that support is through communicating with God, and the only I can do that is to first have a personal relationship with Christ. Once you have trusted Jesus as Savior, God speaks to you from the Bible through the Holy Spirit, and you are able to understand His message. The way we speak to Him is through prayer. We affirm our faith by being a part of a church and seeking fellowship with our brothers and sisters in Christ.

FAST FACT:

Michael was a first-round pick of Montreal in the 1993 draft.

There is nothing any of us has done to earn salvation or a relationship with the Father. It is only through God's grace that we can have eternal life. I apply God's grace to my life every day by trying to live the example Christ set for me.

One of my favorite Bible passages is Romans 12:1–2. It says, "I beseech you therefore, brethren, by the mercies of God, that you present your bodies a living sacrifice, holy, acceptable to God, which is your reasonable service. And do not be conformed to this world, but be transformed by the renewing of your mind, that you may prove what is that good and acceptable and perfect will of God" (NKJV).

As Christians, we must follow God's guidance and the support He gives to us in the Word. By staying in the Word and in prayer, we are able to realize God's will for our lives. Through this relationship with Christ, I have learned (and this is so important) that nothing in this world is greater than God and His love for me.

He is with me in the good times and the bad.

—MICHAEL BARRETT

FOLLOW THROUGH

As you consider what you've thought about, participated in, and prepared for in the past week, can you agree with Michael that nothing you did was more important than nurturing your relationship with Christ?

From the Playbook: Read Romans 12.

NO. 71 JOE GIRARDI When Joe and Kim Girardi had to move from Chicago to New York early in his career, he was not happy. Didn't want to go to the Big Apple. Struggled, actually. "Kim had to keep telling me that 'God has a plan for you.'" In 2008, Girardi was named manager of the Yankees.

72. THE STREAK

"Three times a day [Daniel] got down on his knees and prayed."

DANIEL 6:10

In 2007, Cal Ripken, one of the most beloved players in baseball history, was inducted into the Baseball Hall of Fame in Cooperstown, New York. Ripken, who played all of his 21 seasons in a Baltimore Orioles jersey, certainly had Hall-worthy stats: 431 home runs, 1,695 RBI, 1982 American League Rookie of the Year, two-time AL MVP and Gold Glove winner, 19-time All-Star.

But what the Iron Man will be known for most is The Streak—playing in 2,632 consecutive games, a tally that far surpassed Lou Gehrig's seemingly untouchable mark of 2,130 games.

FAST FACT:

Cal Ripken was named on a record 537 Hall of Fame ballots.

Did you ever consider the value of going on a spiritual streak? Think of it. We are to be constantly in prayer, which is essential to our spiritual growth and effectiveness. Prayer is our lifeblood, giving us the unique opportunity to worship, confess, thank, and supplicate with our heavenly Father. Wouldn't it be exciting to be on a 2,632-consecutive-day prayer streak?

Take a look at the sterling example of Daniel in Daniel 6:10: "Three times a day he got down on his knees and prayed, giving thanks to his God." In fact, Daniel's commitment to prayer was so evident that even his jealous peers in the Persian government noticed it.

First Thessalonians 5:17 implores us to "pray continually." Ephesians 6:18 says, "Pray in the Spirit on all occasions with all kinds of prayers and requests." And the Gospels record numerous times when Jesus himself went off to quiet places to pray.

Clearly, daily prayer is a streak that we, as God's children, should never break. How's your streak going?

—Joshua Cooley

FOLLOW THROUGH

Commit to a plan to read through the Psalms, noting how David and other psalmists prayed to God.

From the Playbook: Read Matthew 6:5–14.

NO. 72 MARK TEIXEIRA Most baseball players would do anything to have one season like Mark Teixeira's version of 2005 with the Texas Rangers. In that season, he hit 43 home runs, batted in 144 runs, and hit .301. He made the All-Star team, won a Gold Glove, and led the AL in total bases with 370. Even then, he needed a break. "You need a time out to spend reflecting on your life and your life with God."

73. THE CAROUSEL

*But seek first [God's] kingdom and his righteousness,
and all these things will be given to you."*

MATTHEW 6:33

One of my daughters loves to ride on the carousel. When the gate opens, it's a race to "her" horse. She loves every bit of it. When the ride is over, she is not happy. The first words out of her mouth are, "Can I go again?" One minute she's up, and the next she's down. She must continue to ride the carousel until she is totally satisfied.

FAST FACT:
Russ Ortiz pitched in the 2002 World Series while with the San Francisco Giants.

At that moment, my daughter's search for joy is a beautifully decorated horse. After that, it's always a different decorated horse. A carousel looks pretty and fun and has many horses to choose from, but when you think about it, all it does is go around in a circle. And you end up at the same place you started. When that ride ends and she wants to do it again, sometimes it costs something.

Getting to the pinnacle of any profession doesn't happen over night. You sweat, you ache, you cry, and you stick with it. But we want satisfaction now! We will try many beautifully decorated things to bring us that satisfaction. Sometimes we end up having to pay a hefty price for it too.

Psalm 37:4 has a cure for that merry-go-round routine. "Delight yourself in the Lord," the verse says, "and he will give you the desires of your heart." If we trust in God and seek His kingdom first, His righteousness can be ours. His desires will become our desires. And we won't need to ride the carousel of unfulfilled wishes anymore.

—Russ Ortiz

FOLLOW THROUGH

What are some things you can honestly say you substitute for your relationship with Jesus? Do those things complete you? What are some ways you can move toward a closer relationship with Jesus?

From the Playbook: Read Galatians 5.

NO. 73 EDGARDO ALFONZO The Venezuelan infielder shined the brightest in the last two years of the twentieth century when he hit over .300 and had 367 hits for the New York Mets. He had become a Christian a few years previous when Carlos Baerga showed him the way. "At Turner Field in Atlanta, I accepted Jesus Christ as my Savior," Alfonzo recalls. He retired in 2006 with a lifetime BA of .284.

74. GIVING IT YOUR BEST

Strike Zone:
Sharing the faith

"Always be prepared to give an answer."
1 PETER 3:15

In order to give the best effort we are capable of, we are required to prepare properly.

As a pitcher, I prepared diligently for each start so I could perform at the top of my game. I prepared myself physically, mentally, and emotionally on my day to pitch but also on the four days in between. I constructed a "game plan," or strategy, against the team I would face. If I was well prepared, I could approach each start with full confidence. If I neglected this responsibility or did not give a full effort, I struggled and was not able to pitch to the best of my ability.

FAST FACT:
Mike Maroth was nominated for the Major League Baseball Clemente Award (for community service) in 2006.

The concept applies to our witness as a follower of Christ as well. Preparation of our testimony affects not only our personal relationship with the Lord but also our ability to influence others for Christ. If we are not equipped with the Word, we may not be prepared to help others discover a personal relationship with God through Jesus. Giving an answer to what we believe demands that we read the Bible and communicate with God through prayer on a daily basis.

God does not want us to keep our faith to ourselves. He desires for us to share what Christ has done in our lives with those who do not know Him and those who need to be encouraged. When we do, we give others the opportunity to know Jesus Christ as their Lord and Savior.

Commit to proper preparation, and you will be confident in sharing the hope God has given you.

—MIKE MAROTH

FOLLOW THROUGH

Have you ever written your testimony so that when you have a chance to share it with someone you'll know what to say? Try it this week. Then read it to a Christian friend who can help you say it even better.

From the Playbook: Read Paul the apostle's testimony in Acts 22.

NO. 74 STEVE BEDROSIAN As a former Cy Young Award winner, Steve Bedrosian could rest on his laurels, but he has decided to stay active in his community. He lives out his faith through working with young people as an assistant coach at his children's high school, and he serves on that school's board. Bedrosian won the NL Cy Young Award in 1987 with 40 saves and an ERA of 2.83.

75. LOOK WHO'S WATCHING

My life is an example to many, because you have been my strength and protection."

PSALM 71:7 (NLT)

Writing in Psalm 71, the psalmist explained that he had a responsibility to be an example to others. It's something all of us as believers should recognize.

I realize that people watch the lives of professional athletes closely, but nobody watches a person as closely as his or her own family does.

In March 2006, my wife Alicia and I were blessed with the birth of our daughter, Reagan Lucille. There is something about the birth of your own child that puts things in perspective. Family has always been very important to us. Knowing that we now have a daughter of our own, Alicia and I want to be the example to her that our parents were to us. That starts by teaching her that God loves her and has a wonderful plan for her life.

FAST FACT:
Brandon and Alicia met in college at the University of Kentucky, where Brandon played baseball.

Because of the time away from home my career requires, I will have to take every available opportunity to be there for Reagan and set a good example for her. Also, I will need to pray for Alicia in her role as mom and as she continues to encourage me during the long baseball season.

The writer of Psalm 71 had confidence because God had been his "strength and protection" in the past. God can give each of us the same strength and protection as we seek to be good examples for those who are watching us.

—BRANDON WEBB

FOLLOW THROUGH

If you are married and have children, discuss as a couple the ways you can be there for each other and your children. Everybody's situation is different, so work out how you should make this happen in your family.

From the Playbook: Read Deuteronomy 6:4–9.

NO. 75 SCOTT BROSIUS While a minor leaguer trying to crack in to the bigs—and before he got his big shot with the New York Yankees, Brosius was led to faith in Jesus Christ by a friend, Rocky Coyle, and others. "God placed a lot of people in my life at the right time who led me to the decision to trust Jesus." Brosius' big moment came in 1998 when he hit back-to-back World Series home runs—just the sixth Yankee ever to do that. He was named the MVP of that Series.

76. DON'T GO IT ALONE

"As iron sharpens iron, so one man sharpens another."
PROVERBS 27:17

Just as a sword cannot be shaped by itself, neither can we. There are many tools and instruments that a sword must rely on in order for it to be made strong and sharp. The process takes time, but the end result is well worth it.

Do you have someone that you can rely on to sharpen you?

A sports season is tough, whatever level you play at. The ups and downs, the travel—it's a grind every year. You get worn out. Having one or more teammates or friends who can lift you up during the grueling season makes a huge difference. Fellowship is crucial.

FAST FACT:
Russ Ortiz won 21 games for the Atlanta Braves in 2003.

When I played with the Atlanta Braves in 2003 and 2004, I was able to team up with an awesome group of guys. We developed a fellowship group that met daily all throughout Spring Training and the season. We helped each other through encouragement, teaching, and prayer. We were a tool and an instrument for one another to help shape our thinking and to lead us closer to our Savior Jesus Christ. When I look back on those two seasons, I am thankful to have had some guys to call on when it got tough and when I struggled with something.

I encourage you to find someone who can sharpen you and with whom you can do the same. The Christian life, like a long sports season, is hard. We all need someone to hold us accountable so we can stay strong and sharp.

—RUSS ORTIZ

FOLLOW THROUGH

What person or persons can you call on when things get tough? Who can you think of that you can encourage today?

From the Playbook: Read 2 Timothy 1–2:13.

NO. 76 RUSS ORTIZ On the bill of his baseball cap, pitcher Russ Ortiz liked to write Bible verses to remind him of his true purpose in life. That intrigued sportswriters, but Ortiz wasn't doing it for them. "As a Christian athlete," he said, "I play for an audience of one. I play for Christ." And Ortiz played well. From 1999 to 2004, Ortiz won 99 games, including 21 in 2003.

77. MR. OCTOBER'S HIP

"Who despises the day of small things?"
ZECHARIAH 4:10

Every baseball fan knows about Reggie Jackson's World Series heroics, but I would guess that not many remember his apparent "confusion" on a strange play in 1978. Reggie was on first base in Game 4 with the New York Yankees down two games to one. The Dodgers were about to turn an easy double play to end the inning when Reggie, halfway down the line, stopped and leaned his hip into the relay. The ball sailed into foul territory, and Thurman Munson scored.

What happened next was classic. Reggie looked around as if he didn't know what to do. Should he go to second? Back to first?

It was all part of his plan to use one little move to change the direction of the game. And it worked.

Reggie had a tremendous awareness of the importance of little things. He had saved his team only one out, but the Yankees scored, went on to seize control of that game, and eventually won the Series.

FAST FACT:

Reggie Jackson struck out a record 2,597 times in his career, but he hit 563 home runs and 10 more in the World Series— including four in a row over two games in 1977.

It may have been a little thing for a small boy to give his lunch to Jesus. And it may have been a little thing that Andrew brought the boy to Jesus. But what Jesus did was huge. He turned one small lunch into a feast for 5,000. And because of this, many would come to believe that Jesus was the Messiah.

166

Perhaps you're thinking that your small contribution doesn't matter. Don't believe it. Small things count for God's big purposes.

Home run heroics are great, but it's little things that win games, and eventually World Series. And sometimes it's the little things that can accomplish big things for God.

—Tim Gustafson

FOLLOW THROUGH

Do I ever think my efforts don't matter? What can God do with my work when I do it for Him? What "little things" should I be doing to serve Him?

From the Playbook: Read John 6:1–15.

NO. 77 RICO PETROCELLI At one time, he held the record for home runs by a shortstop in a season (40). He was a key player in one of the greatest World Series ever played (1975). And he was a Boston Red Sox icon. But what really changed life for Rico was when his wife was diagnosed with cancer. That led to Petrocelli turning his life over to Jesus—and his wife beat the cancer. "There are times you worry, but instead of going on your own merits, you can go to Christ," he says.

78. A HEART FOR OTHERS

"A generous man will prosper; he who refreshes others will himself be refreshed."

PROVERBS 11:25

Major league money didn't change pitcher Woody Williams and his wife Kimberli. They had servants' hearts when they were bouncing around in the International League, and they had servants' hearts when Williams was a successful major league pitcher.

Rob Picciolo, a coach for the San Diego Padres during Woody's time with that National League club, said the pitcher galvanized an effort to reward the trainers. As a result, team management awarded salary increases to the trainers. Williams also raised funds to buy a vehicle for both of the clubhouse assistants. One of the assistants later called Woody and said, "I think about you every time I open that door."

FAST FACT:
Woody Williams won 18 games for the St. Louis Cardinals in 2003.

"In my 13 years in the big leagues with the Padres, this is the one player who demonstrated an appreciation for trainers and clubhouse kids more than any player I've ever been associated with," Picciolo says. "He's got a good heart."

David Fisher, former Baseball Chapel representative to the Toronto Blue Jays, says Kimberli not only led that team's players' wives in a food-bank collection but she also led someone to faith in Jesus outside Rogers Centre, the team's home ballpark.

Kimberli says that when she sees someone in need and feels God is leading her to give, she helps that person.

One time Woody and Kimberli were driving to their kids' elementary school when they passed an intersection and saw a van parked on the shoulder. There was a man with a teddy bear and a sign, WILL TRADE THIS BEAR FOR GAS. They stopped, and she gave him twenty dollars.

We can all find ways to do this—to stop what we're doing and help others in Jesus' name.

—RICK WEBER

FOLLOW THROUGH

Whether we are rich or poor, we have a responsibility to meet the needs of others. Who do you know who needs a bit of assistance from you?

From the Playbook: Read 2 Corinthians 8:1–15.

NO. 78 LARRY HISLE Quiet. Powerful. That's Larry Hisle. One of the most honorable men who ever donned a baseball uniform, Hisle is not defined by his 166 career home runs and his .273 average. No, he is defined by the multitude of kids he has mentored, one on one, trying to show them that life does not have to be about anger, drugs, and gangs. "I truly believe that if God has given me any gift at all, it's the ability to work with young people," says Hisle, who hit 34 home runs with 115 RBI with Milwaukee in 1978.

79. YOU GOTTA BELIEVE

*"If you believe, you will receive whatever
you ask for in prayer."*

MATTHEW 21:22

At the end of August 1973, the New York Mets were 10 games under .500 and fading fast from the National League play-off picture.

Sensing a need for a quick turnaround, pitcher Tug McGraw pleaded with his teammates to have some faith. "You gotta believe," he said. How did the Mets respond? Just by winning 21 of their final 29 games to finish with an 82-79 record. The Mets then shocked the powerful Cincinnati Reds in the NLCS to reach the World Series.

Pretty gutsy stuff, huh? And yet, it all started with a little belief.

In Matthew 21, Jesus gives us a pretty powerful picture of what faith can do. If we do not doubt, Jesus says, you can say to a mountain, "Go, throw yourself into the sea" and it will be done (v. 21). Imagine the power Jesus is referring to with this illustration!

That's the kind of confidence Jesus wants us to have when we turn to Him in prayer. Jesus doesn't want us to go to Him filled with doubt and lacking the faith that He's powerful enough to meet our needs. All He asks from us is faith.

FAST FACT:
Tug McGraw, father of singer Tim McGraw, threw the last pitch in the Phillies' 1980 World Series-clinching win.

If faith in each other can help the Mets, imagine what faith in Jesus can do for us.

—Jeff Arnold

FOLLOW THROUGH

Is there something you've been meaning to turn over to God, but doubt has kept you from asking? Why not take a minute today to amp up your faith level and go to Jesus in confidence, believing that He will come through on His promise to give you what He believes is best for you.

From the Playbook: Read Matthew 21.

NO. 79 SEAN CASEY The Mayor. He can talk a leg off a piano bench. Anytime a player arrived at first when Casey was there with a glove, conversation ensued. But he didn't just talk a good game. He also hit .300 or better six times in the majors. "One of the greatest testimonies you can give as a Christian is the way you live your life," said the Mayor.

80. THE OWNER IS HERE

> "Yours, O Lord, is the kingdom; you are
> exalted as head over all."
>
> 1 CHRONICLES 29:11

In my third full season as a professional baseball player, I was stuck in Double A and not doing so well. Then in one week I raised my batting average about 30 points. Feeling good about myself, I was just playing and not trying too hard. Suddenly, everything was coming easily.

That all changed when in the first inning of a game my team was informed that the general manager and the owner of the big club were at our game. I tensed up, and I had a terrible game. I wish I could say that this was a rare occurrence, but it wasn't. Every time a scout would show up in high school, I would try so hard to impress him, and I would fail terribly. Failing was the exact thing I was so afraid to do in front of these men.

FAST FACT:
Matt's first major-league walk-off hit helped the Braves defeat the Marlins 4-3 in 11 innings on May 16, 2006.

After that Double-A game we had a fifteen-hour bus ride, so I had plenty of time to think about how poorly I had played. Sometime around three in the morning I got out my Bible and read the verse above (please read it completely in your Bible). I realized that I trusted God to rule the heavens and things that are far off, but the verse says, "for everything in heaven and earth is yours" (v. 11). I had to change my thinking. I had to realize who the true Owner was. He owns my job as a baseball player, He owns my family, and He even owns my next breath.

While we are commanded to honor those in authority over us and respect them, it is also clear that we are not to fear any man. Again, we know the Owner, and He is for us.

Now, let's go out and live life relaxed—giving God our very best.

—MATT DIAZ

FOLLOW THROUGH

Who intimidates you? Is it a boss? A spouse or parent? Is their intimidation a result of not trusting God to rule everything in heaven and on earth? Keep a list today of all the people you truly aren't yourself around, and pray that God will give you the courage to respect them but not fear them.

From the Playbook: Read Deuteronomy 1:15–17 and see what God tells these new leaders of the Promised Land to do with tough situations.

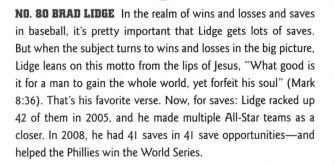

NO. 80 BRAD LIDGE In the realm of wins and losses and saves in baseball, it's pretty important that Lidge gets lots of saves. But when the subject turns to wins and losses in the big picture, Lidge leans on this motto from the lips of Jesus, "What good is it for a man to gain the whole world, yet forfeit his soul" (Mark 8:36). That's his favorite verse. Now, for saves: Lidge racked up 42 of them in 2005, and he made multiple All-Star teams as a closer. In 2008, he had 41 saves in 41 save opportunities—and helped the Phillies win the World Series.

81. WHAT IS GOD THINKING?

"'For I know the thoughts that I think toward you,'
says the LORD."
JEREMIAH 29:11 (NKJV)

Have you ever gone through life wondering what God is thinking? Do you ever say to yourself, "God, are You up there paying attention to me? Do you see the turmoil I am in, and do you care?"

I have asked those questions many times. I have even looked up Jeremiah 29:11 ("'For I know the thoughts that I think toward you,' says the Lord, 'thoughts of peace and not of evil'") and quoted it over and over again to encourage myself in this spiritual journey that at times feels like quicksand. It feels like quicksand more often than I think it should.

FAST FACT:
Jeremy Affeldt made his major league debut on April 6, 2002.

I remember flipping my Bible open to Jeremiah 29:11 one time when I needed to hear God's thoughts toward me. I remember deciding to read further down the page to verse 13. In this spiritual journey I began to understand what God is after. No matter what happens in life, no matter how good or bad things are, we wonder what he wants from us.

Well, verse 13 says He wants us to chase after Him. He wants us to crave Him with all of our hearts. When we do that, we will find Him. We will find His smile, it will warm our souls, and we will find solid ground to walk on and a hand to help us up when we are sinking.

Sometimes the answers aren't always spelled out on the wall, but our questions will be answered, and His Word never returns to Him void. God will come through, and we will rejoice in Him for He is so good!

—JEREMY AFFELDT

FOLLOW THROUGH

What have you recently thought God's thoughts are toward you? Have you ever considered the Jeremiah 29:13 concept that God wants you to chase after Him—to pursue Him in your pursuit of happiness?

From the Playbook: Read Jeremiah 29.

NO. 81 BOB BOONE How does one family get four major league baseball players across three generations? "Call it a gift from God," says Bob Boone, who was second in the line behind his dad, Ray. Bob's sons Adam and Bret also had successful MLB careers. Boone appeared in a remarkable 2,225 games as a catcher during a 20-year career.

82. A SPIT IN THE FACE

"Miriam and Aaron began to talk against Moses."

NUMBERS 12:1

Roberto Alomar was one of the best baseball players of his era. But his reputation will forever by stained be one thoughtless, spur-of-the-moment act during the last weekend of the 1996 season. Upset with the decision of a home-plate umpire, Alomar spit in the ump's face. With that one disgusting move, he became the object of criticism throughout the sports world.

He later apologized, and he and the umpire even became friends. But the damage was done. By one uncontrolled moment of retaliation, Alomar placed his good name in jeopardy.

Miriam, Moses' sister, suffered a public humiliation of her own. In a moment of thoughtlessness, Miriam criticized God's choice of her brother Moses as leader. God, who selected Moses to direct the Israelites, grew angry with Miriam's criticism and struck her with leprosy.

FAST FACT:

Roberto Alomar had a career batting average of .300, and he retired in 2004 with 2,724 hits.

When Moses asked God to heal her of this flesh-eating disease, the heavenly Father gave Moses this analogy:

"If her father had spit in her face, would she not have been in disgrace for seven days?" (Numbers 12:14). Then he told Moses to send her outside the camp for seven days. Her public criticism resulted in a public humiliation. She had rebuked God harshly, and her punishment was swift and clear.

Had Roberto Alomar taken just three seconds to think of his act, he never would have soiled his reputation by humiliating the umpire. Had Miriam taken the time to consider the impact of her criticism of God's prophet, she could have spared herself some intense pain.

We have a responsibility under God to act nobly and do the right thing—and to avoid actions we will regret. Every moment, let's consecrate ourselves to a life of honor and respect before our living, loving God.

—DAVE BRANON

FOLLOW THROUGH

In the past three days, what are two things you did that you regret now? Would a 10-second prayer at the time have stopped you from those actions? Is that a good plan for future decisions?

From the Playbook: Read Numbers 12.

NO. 82 PHIL REGAN How'd you like to be called The Vulture? Before the age of relief specialists, Regan was a relief pitcher. One season, pitching in relief exclusively he won 14 games and lost one with 21 saves and 48 games finished. You don't see stats like that anymore. Once Regan had been wrongly accused of throwing a spitter. Later, the umpire recanted, saying of Regan, "He's a fine Christian gentleman." And so he was during and after his playing career, which ended in 1972.

83. THE RED SOX AND ETERNITY

"The eternal God is your refuge, and underneath are the everlasting arms."

DEUTERONOMY 33:27

Imagine having to wait 86 years for something?

In baseball-crazed New England, that's exactly how long fans of the Boston Red Sox endured between World Series championships. The team, most believed, was cursed after Red Sox owner Harry Frazee sold Babe Ruth to the hated New York Yankees in 1920 for $100,000 to finance his girlfriend's stage play.

FAST FACT:

The Yankees won 26 World Series in the time between the fifth and sixth Series won by the Red Sox.

The Red Sox, who had won five World Series between 1903 and 1918, didn't win again until finally claiming the world title in 2004, ending what for many seemed like an eternal wait.

But in God's time, what seems to be an eternity for us is actually no time at all. In Deuteronomy 33, God is described as being eternal—his arms everlasting—as in forever.

How cool is it to know that God's presence knows no time and that as long as He keeps us on earth His presence in our lives, once we've accepted Him, knows no boundaries. His love and support are always there for us, a guarantee that gives us great peace, knowing that when we call upon the Lord, there's no question that He will always be there for us. Not just for the next 10 years—not just for the next 50.

Our God is eternal, and one day we will spend the rest of eternity with Him.

And unlike Red Sox fans, who thought their wait for a winner would never come to an end, our relationship to the ever-lasting Savior will absolutely never run out.

—JEFF ARNOLD

FOLLOW THROUGH

Why not take use your quiet time today to thank God for His everlasting qualities in your life. Think of a time when you weren't sure God was there and when you forgot about His eternal presence—and contrast that with the truth of Deuteronomy 33:27. God never goes away from us and never will. Why not tell Him what that means to you.

From the Playbook: Read Deuteronomy 33.

NO. 83 MIKE STANLEY Stanley Tools get the job done. Stanley the baseball player did too. Through hard work and tough play, Stanley constructed a career in which he hit 187 home runs and banged out 1,138 hits. A one-time All-Star, he hit more than 20 home runs four times in his career. He worked hard off the field as well. "It takes a lot of effort to stay in the Word every day and keep yourself close to Christ," he says.

84. COMMANDED COURAGE

Strike Zone:
Living courageously

"Be strong and courageous."

JOSHUA 1:9

Joshua was a man of God who was taking over for Moses. His job was to succeed Moses and guide the children of Israel into the Promised Land. Now, taking over for Moses could have been a little intimidating to Joshua. After all, God used Moses to stand up to Pharaoh, lead the Israelites out of Egypt, part the Red Sea, and conduct many other miracles along the way. There were probably around a million Israelites at the time, and Joshua was fearful of his monumental task.

FAST FACT:
Scott Fletcher played from 1981 through 1995 for six major league teams.

But God knew Joshua's heart. He knew that in order for the job to get done and for the new leader to be successful, his attitude had to change. That's why God didn't *ask* Joshua to be strong and courageous. He didn't *suggest* to him to be strong and courageous. He *commanded* him.

There is a huge difference.

I found that many times as athletes, we can become fearful about many things: Fear of what the coach is thinking about us. Fear of failing. Fear of our opponent. Fear of our environment.

But we have an advantage over fear—athlete or not. You see, God knows what it is going to take to overcome the situation. He's the creator of life.

Whenever fear or doubt tries to creep into our thoughts or hearts, we need to do what God commanded Joshua to do: Start being strong and courageous! When we do, fear and doubt will leave and victory will march right in.

—SCOTT FLETCHER

FOLLOW THROUGH

What fear am I facing today? Or what fear do I face over and over? If I listen to God's command to be strong and courageous, how do I put that into practice against fear?

From the Playbook: Read Joshua 1.

NO. 84 JIM SUNDBERG After catching in the majors for 16 seasons (three All-Star games, seven Gold Gloves), Sundberg has done many things. But among the most rewarding was putting on a different mask: a surgical mask. He went on a missions trip to Guatemala to give dental help to needy folks there. "It was one of the most rewarding things I've ever done."

85. THE BEST REVENGE

*"Vindicate me in your righteousness, O Lord my God;
do not let them gloat over me."*

PSALM 35:24

The setting was the "Homer Dome" in Minneapolis. The Detroit Tigers held an early 4-0 lead on the hometown Twins when Minnesota loaded the bases against Mike Moore. Dave Winfield, he of the rippling biceps and future Hall-of-Fame credentials, dug in—cocked bat twitching like a lion's tail.

Moore's first pitch sailed directly for Winfield's chin. He dropped like a bad stock, narrowly avoiding an RBI the hard way. The crowd's mood, already electric, escalated to near nuclear meltdown. Winfield didn't glare, didn't threaten, didn't yell. He simply got back in the batter's box and launched the next pitch into the left field seats to tie the game.

FAST FACT:
Eleven of Winfield's 465 career home runs were grand slams.

Wouldn't it be nice if all our perceived injustices were remedied so promptly? But as so often happens in life, justice seems slow, even nonexistent. It's an age-old problem—the result of living in a fallen world.

It was no mere baseball game King David was playing when he wrote Psalm 35. He was engaged in a life-and-death struggle with those who "hid their net for me without cause" (v. 7). Despite his reputation as a mighty warrior, David didn't seek to correct the situation himself. Rather, he called out to

God with surprisingly candid words: "Awake, and rise to my defense!" he urged the Lord. "Contend for me" (v. 23).

David's heart-wrenching song reveals a man not unlike us. He longed for vindication (vv. 24, 27) and yearned for the day when those who pursued him unjustly would be "put to shame and confusion" (v. 26). He knew his vindication would arrive—in God's good time.

God's justice is always so much better than ours. Let's learn to leave any perceived vindication in His holy hands.

—Tim Gustafson

FOLLOW THROUGH

What is usually your first reaction when you are wronged? Do you ever ask God's Holy Spirit to help you leave vengeance and justice to Him? How is this a sign of strength and not of weakness?

From the Playbook: Read Psalm 35:19–28.

NO. 85 SCOTT SANDERSON Some fortunate baseball players find ways to keep themselves in the game after their careers on the field end. For Sanderson, who pitched for 19 seasons in the majors—winning 163 games and striking out 1,611 hitters—that way to keep involved is as a sports agent. "I felt like God was calling me to stay in the game of baseball by serving today's players. It's a great mission field."

86. LIFT THAT BURDEN!

*"Then Joseph said to his brothers: . . . 'Do not be distressed
and do not be angry with yourselves for selling me here,
because it was to save lives that God sent me ahead of you.'"*

GENESIS 45:4–5

It was the last weekend of the 1964 major league baseball season. Bill Valentine was umpiring a game between the Detroit Tigers and the New York Yankees.

Dave Wickersham was pitching for Detroit, and he had 19 victories for the season. One more win would bring him to 20—a sure sign of stardom for any pitcher. Wickersham, whose best season for wins was 12 in 1963, was one victory from the recognition of being one of the game's top pitchers.

In the seventh inning, with the score tied at 1-1, the umpire got into an argument with Detroit's Norm Cash. Wickersham walked over and tapped Valentine on the shoulder to get his attention. Touching an umpire is against the rules, so Valentine kicked Wickersham out of the game—depriving him of his chance for a 20-win season.

FAST FACT:

Dave Wickersham went 68-57 in his 10-year major league pitching career from 1960 through 1969.

For the next 39 years, Valentine lived with a gnawing regret for booting the pitcher in that split-second decision. But he doesn't carry that regret anymore. A few years ago, Wickersham wrote the umpire a note, telling Valentine that he was right in his decision and that Wickersham held no hard feelings. That note lifted a weight from Valentine's shoulders.

In Genesis 45, Joseph lifted a burden of guilt from the shoulders of his brothers, who had sold him into slavery—something far more serious than a simple misunderstanding. Joseph set the example for us all with his open-handed gesture toward his siblings.

Is there someone who needs to hear a forgiving word from you? Go ahead. Lift that burden! You'll both feel better—and God will be glorified.

—DAVE BRANON

FOLLOW THROUGH

Who are two people longing to hear a gentle word of forgiveness and compassion from you? What is stopping you from lifting their burden? Is it time to set up a time to talk to them?

From the Playbook: Read Genesis 45:1–15.

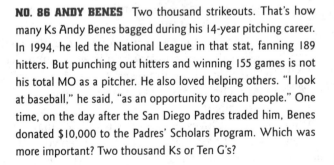

NO. 86 ANDY BENES Two thousand strikeouts. That's how many Ks Andy Benes bagged during his 14-year pitching career. In 1994, he led the National League in that stat, fanning 189 hitters. But punching out hitters and winning 155 games is not his total MO as a pitcher. He also loved helping others. "I look at baseball," he said, "as an opportunity to reach people." One time, on the day after the San Diego Padres traded him, Benes donated $10,000 to the Padres' Scholars Program. Which was more important? Two thousand Ks or Ten G's?

87. ASTERISKS AND JUSTICE

"The eyes of the Lord are on the righteous."
PSALM 34:15

Billy Crystal's movie *61* tracked Roger Maris' thrilling—and tortured—pursuit of Babe Ruth's fabled home run record. Sportswriters, not wanting the Babe's record to fall to anyone not named "Mickey Mantle," hounded Maris throughout the 1961 season. Even though Maris eclipsed Ruth's record, an asterisk appeared next to his name in the record books. The record was somehow "tainted" because he played in a slightly longer season.

That asterisk has subsequently been removed. But ironically, there's now another asterisk in certain record books for the 1961 season. Check the *ESPN Sports Almanac* under "batting champions" for that year. You'll find a star next to Norm Cash's name. It seems the tall Texan admitted to using a corked bat for the entire season! Now *that's* a tainted title.

FAST FACT:
Except for 1961 when he batted .361, Norm Cash never hit higher than .286.

Baseball gives us just a few examples of the way things often work in this world. Injustice is rampant. Those in power reward their favorites. And cheating isn't cheating as long as you don't get caught.

"Whoever of you loves life and desires to see many good days," wrote David before he became king, "keep your tongue from evil and your lips from speaking lies. Turn from evil and do good" (Psalm 34:12–13). His words should comfort us, because the same God who expects us to behave righteously also has His eyes on us for our protection.

"The face of the Lord is against those who do evil" (v. 16). But when the righteous cry out to God, "The Lord hears them; he delivers them from all their troubles" (v. 17).

God's record book needs no asterisks. He will right all wrongs.

—Tim Gustafson

FOLLOW THROUGH

When was the last time I was tempted to cheat? What did I do? How could I resist the temptation? Do I live my life as though God sees me? Do I care more about what others think than what God thinks? Why is that?

From the Playbook: Read Psalm 34:11–22.

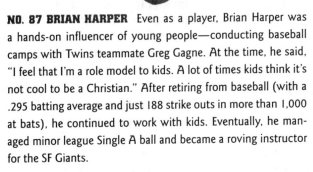

NO. 87 BRIAN HARPER Even as a player, Brian Harper was a hands-on influencer of young people—conducting baseball camps with Twins teammate Greg Gagne. At the time, he said, "I feel that I'm a role model to kids. A lot of times kids think it's not cool to be a Christian." After retiring from baseball (with a .295 batting average and just 188 strike outs in more than 1,000 at bats), he continued to work with kids. Eventually, he managed minor league Single A ball and became a roving instructor for the SF Giants.

88. DON'T PUT YOUR SIGN DOWN

Strike Zone:
Remaining faithful

"By faith ... [Abraham and Sarah] considered him faithful who had made the promise."

HEBREWS 11:11

Remember the "We Believe" signs the Red Sox faithful held up during the 2004 World Series? You didn't see many of them at the end of Game 3 of the ALCS. After being pounded by the Yankees 19-8, and because the Sox were down three games to none, the fans abandoned the "We Believe" signs.

The only thing most fans believed at that point was that Boston's wait for a World Series championship would be longer than the 86 years they had already endured.

Incredibly, the Red Sox came back and beat New York four straight times, and after sweeping the Cardinals in the World Series, the wait was finally over. Sox owner John Henry said, "All of our fans waited their entire lives for this."

In some ways, that is a parable of the Christian life. Faith sometimes involves long, difficult delays. We often have to wait for God to act on His promises to us. And there are times when we're tempted to take down our "We Believe" signs.

In Hebrews 11, one of the marks of the faith of Abraham and Sarah was that they believed even though they had an excruciating wait. God had promised them a son, and even though they had plenty of reasons to toss aside their "We Believe" signs, they didn't. After 40 years, God delivered on His promise and Isaac was born.

It may seem like you have reasons to put your sign down. But you also have a God with a perfect reputation of faithfulness. That should give you reason to hang on to your sign and hold it high.

—Brian Hettinga

FOLLOW THROUGH

Are you waiting for test results from the doctor? Are you waiting for a friend or family member to turn to God? Are you waiting . . .? Hang on to your "We Believe" sign, and look for ways God will prove Himself faithful.

From the Playbook: Read Hebrews 11:8–16.

NO. 88 LINDY MCDANIEL Not many pitchers hang around the big leagues as long as Lindy McDaniel did. From 1955 until 1975, McDaniel donned the uniforms of five different teams, appeared in almost 1,000 games as a pitcher, and ended with 141 wins and 172 saves. And how did he do it? According to his Web site, through "a strong belief in God—especially during times of adversity."

89. WILLING AND ABLE

"[Isaiah] said, 'Here am I. Send me!'"
ISAIAH 6:8

Kirk Gibson could barely walk. With a painful leg injury keeping him out of the Los Angeles Dodgers' World Series lineup in 1988, Gibson was in the training room in the bottom of the ninth inning during Game 1. The Dodgers trailed the Oakland A's 4-3 with two out and a runner on first. Gibson hobbled up the dugout tunnel and told Dodgers manager Tommy Lasorda to let him hit. With one swing and one excruciating jog around the bases, Gibson gave the Dodgers a victory that led to a world championship.

Pretty dramatic stuff, huh?

And yet, all it took was one person to stand up and say, "I'll get the job done."

That's all Isaiah did when he had a vision in which he saw the Lord sitting on a throne looking for a messenger to deliver some important words to His people.

FAST FACT:
Kirk Gibson went to Michigan State University on a football scholarship.

In that situation, recorded in Isaiah 6, it would have been easy for Isaiah to say to himself, 'There's got to be somebody better than me—someone who's a better speaker or a better leader."

But instead, he told the Lord, "Here am I. Send me!" (v. 8).

As Lasorda had done with Gibson, God chose to give His willing servant an important task at a pivotal time. Willingness is all God wants from us. He desires so much for us to want to be used by Him. He wants us to believe in the gifts He has given us, trust Him, and tell Him, "Use me. I'm ready."

—Jeff Arnold

FOLLOW THROUGH

God has made you unique for a reason, giving you talents He hasn't given anyone else. He has a job for you—it may be big or it may be small—but because you're living for Him and are available to serve, He will bless you for your efforts.

From the Playbook: Read Isaiah 6.

NO. 89 ALVIN DAVIS On April 11 and 13, 1984, Alvin Davis began his big league career with a bang. He hit home runs in each of his first two games. It would prove to be a sign of good things to come; he was the American League Rookie of the Year that season. Davis played in just nine major league seasons, but he made his mark—hitting .280 with 160 home runs. A Christian since he was 12, Davis has said his life is guided by Proverbs 3:5–6.

90. HOLY COW!

"Be holy, because I am holy."
1 PETER 1:16

Legendary baseball announcer Harry Caray made the phrase "Holy Cow" famous. "Holy Cow! He struck him out!" he would say. We also hear people talk about "Holy Toledo!" (If you live there, you know it's not true.)

But when it comes to being truly holy—well, it's a far cry from animals or cities. The concept of being holy is something we need to examine with seriousness and concern. How can we not? Scripture clearly quotes God as saying, "Be holy, because I am holy."

FAST FACT:
Harry Caray was a major league baseball play-by-play announcer from 1945 until 1997.

We also read these pronouncements about holiness in the Bible: "You ought to live holy and godly lives" (2 Peter 3:11). "Make every effort to live in peace with all men and to be holy" (Hebrews 12:14). "God . . . has saved us and called us to a holy life" (2 Timothy 1:8–9).

Sounds monk-like, doesn't it? There is no doubt, though, that God has put holy living out there as a goal we are to reach for—not some unattainable impossibility.

So, what does it mean? Here's what an eighteenth-century Christian writer named William Law said about it: "This, and this alone, is Christianity, a universal holiness in every part of life, a heavenly wisdom in all our actions, not conforming in the spirit and temper of the world but turning all worldly enjoyments into means of piety and devotion to God." Be holy, indeed!

In a society that doesn't think much of Christian piety and devotion to God and His Word, this is a double challenge. But it is possible.

Cows aren't holy and neither is Toledo. But you can be. Go for it.

—DAVE BRANON

FOLLOW THROUGH

Do you equate holy with "no fun" and "boring"? How can you think differently? Do you know anyone whose life seems to be marked by the kind of holiness you'd like to experience?

From the Playbook: Read Hebrews 10:1–10.

NO. 90 WOODY WILLIAMS In 2003, Woody Williams put together his best major league season, winning 18 games and making the All-Star team. Williams won 132 games in a 15-year career that began with him in the bullpen for three seasons. In 2000, he had blood clots surgically removed—a problem that could have ended his career. "It was unbelievable, the power of prayer," he says about how things turned out.

91. SMALL PACKAGE, BIG RESULTS

"The Lord does not look at the things man looks at. Man looks at the outward appearance, but the Lord looks at the heart."

1 SAMUEL 16:7

The list of World Series MVPs includes some of baseball's immortals—players like Sandy Koufax, Frank Robinson, Roberto Clemente, and Reggie Jackson.

Then there's David Eckstein. The St. Louis shortstop etched his name into history in 2006, batting .364 to help the Cardinals beat Detroit in five games.

FAST FACT:
David Eckstein also won a World Series ring with the Angels in 2002.

Averaging less than four home runs a season and with a lifetime batting average in the .285 range, Eckstein is the archetypal underdog. The 5-foot-6, 170-pound player was even a walk-on in college. Yet there he was in October 2006, clutching the MVP trophy after a sterling performance in the Fall Classic. As Eckstein proved, you don't have to be the megastar to accomplish great things. Small packages can deliver big results.

The same is true spiritually. God loves underdogs. Just take a look at Scripture: Moses had a speech impediment, yet he led the Israelites out of Egypt. David rose from being a lowly shepherd to becoming Israel's greatest king. Paul hunted Christians before becoming Christianity's greatest advocate. The list goes on and on.

Jesus himself had a similar aura around him. God Incarnate was born not in a palace but a manger. As an adult, He surrounded Himself not with the rich and famous, but with fishermen, tax collectors, and social castoffs—many of whom went on to spread the gospel after Jesus' resurrection.

The message is clear: It's not our own stature or abilities that make us great in the kingdom of God. It's who we're relying on and what God does through us. As Philippians 4:13 says, "I can do everything through him who gives me strength." Jesus' strength can make the small mighty.

—JOSHUA COOLEY

FOLLOW THROUGH

Contrast the meager start of Moses' ministry (Exodus 4:1–17) to its historic end (Deuteronomy 34) and consider why the difference was so stark.

From the Playbook: Read 2 Corinthians 12:1–10.

NO. 91 DAVE DRAVECKY Imagine how good he could have been! When cancer sidelined him, he was just 30 years old and had already established himself as an All-Star and a top left-handed pitcher. When his arm was amputated in 1989, though, he had to let go of his major league career. He turned his attention to helping others who struggle with life issues, starting Outreach of Hope. In that effort, he has reached more people than he ever could as a player.

92. EIGHT HUNDRED NAMES

"God, the blessed and only Ruler, the King of kings and Lord of lords."

1 TIMOTHY 6:15

It was the late 1970s, and the New York Yankees were at it again.

Baseball's winningest team ever was in the midst of adding to its dynasty by beating the Los Angeles Dodgers in both the 1977 and 1978 World Series. At the center of it all was Reggie Jackson.

FAST FACT:

Reggie Jackson was the first player in major league history to amass 100 or more home runs for three different clubs: the A's, the Yankees, and the Angels.

Jackson, who had previously won a World Series championship with the Oakland A's, became known as Mr. October because of his ability to produce clutch home runs in clutch playoff situations.

He lived up to his name on October 18, 1977, when, against the Dodgers, Reggie slugged three home runs off three straight pitches, helping the Yankees beat LA and eventually win another World Series. Sports fans will always remember Jackson by his well-deserved title: Mr. October.

Did you know that Jesus had nicknames as well? In fact, we can know Jesus by a number of titles, including Prince of Peace, King of kings, and Lord of lords. Did you know that throughout the Bible God is referred to by more than eight hundred titles? Eight hundred! How amazing is that? And the best thing is that the Lord always lives up to each one of His names.

Why not take some time to begin documenting all of the titles held by God as recorded in Scripture. Each is a powerful reminder of some aspect of His greatness and majesty. You'll be amazed by what you learn.

Prince of Peace. King of kings. Lord of lords. And so much more!

—Jeff Arnold

FOLLOW THROUGH

Why not take time out of your day and compile a list of God's titles that mean most to you. Then after you do that, spend some time in prayer, addressing our Lord in those titles. Notice how much more meaningful those names become for you.

From the Playbook: Read Isaiah 9:2–7.

NO. 92 DAMION EASLEY When Damion Easley met Jesus in 1994 while a major leaguer, he figured his career would take off. He figured wrong. He struggled and even was sent to the minors. There, he surrendered even his baseball to the Lord. From then on, he realized that his priority was Jesus first. In a distinguished career, Easley was an All-Star and accumulated more than 1,400 hits. In 1998, he had 27 home runs and 100 RBI for Detroit.

93. TOO MUCH OF
A GOOD THING

"A man is a slave to whatever has mastered him."
2 PETER 2:19

Babe Ruth once devoured 12 hot dogs and gulped down eight bottles of pop between games of a doubleheader. Not surprisingly, he was reportedly rushed to the hospital after the game with a severe case of indigestion. Whoa! No kidding. It reminds me of a famous line from the old Alka-Seltzer commercial, "I can't believe I ate the whole thing."

Hot dogs are as much a part of baseball stadiums as the bleachers, pennants, and scoreboards. As far as I'm concerned, you really haven't fully experienced attending a major league baseball game if you don't consume at least one hot dog and an ice-cold Coke. But as the Bambino discovered, too much of a good thing can turn into a bad thing.

It's called overindulgence. Whether it's food, work, relationships, television, or even baseball, we have all done it. And if were not careful, it can get the best of us. And we're talking about more than an upset stomach or a case of severe heartburn.

Too much of anything, even some things that are good in and of themselves, can turn into a habit that will run and ruin our lives. Whatever it is, it can start to have control over us and

FAST FACT:

Over the course of an average season, major league baseball fans consume about 30 million hot dogs at the old ballpark.

not the other way around. The Bible says that a man "is a slave to whatever has mastered him" (2 Peter 2:19).

But it never has to stay that way. The deeper truth is that those who are in Christ are slaves to something greater than sin—God's law (Romans 7:25). And you can never get too much of that!

—JEFF OLSON

FOLLOW THROUGH

Read Romans 6:11–14. What slavemaster is Paul talking about in this passage? What should prevent us from being a slave to sin?

For Further Reading: Check out www.discoveryseries.org/CB961 *When We Just Can't Stop.*

NO. 93 HAROLD REYNOLDS Slick-fielding infielder Harold Reynolds took home the hardware from 1988 through 1990 as the Gold Glove second baseman in the American League. Two of those years he made the All-Star team. And a year later, he received one of baseball's most honored prizes, the Roberto Clemente Award, which signifies both solid performances on the diamond and outstanding contributions to society. In that regard, Reynolds said, "God has put us as men in a position to take a stand on issues, and we have not done that."

94. TAKE HIM TO THE MOUND

"For God did not give us a spirit of timidity, but a spirit of power, of love and of self-discipline."

2 TIMOTHY 1:7

Do you recall the 2002 World Series? I was with the San Francisco Giants that year. I pitched an ugly Game 2, lasting just two innings and giving up nine runs. After I left the game, I realized I had pitched with fear. I told the Lord, "If I get another shot, it will be with You, and it will be for Your glory."

The Series moved on and after five games, it stood at three wins for us and two for the Angels. We got to Game 6, and I had a second chance.

Athletes cannot compete in fear and be successful. Competing in fear brings doubt. In order for us to compete at the highest level, we need to have trust. As a Christian athlete, I knew that I needed to trust what the Lord can provide.

FAST FACT:
Ortiz was selected by the Giants in the fourth round of the 1995 MLB draft.

In 2 Timothy, Paul tells us what the Lord provides if we walk in His spirit. He is not saying it will earn us any accolades. But he is saying that what the Lord provides is far better than what we can provide.

I pitched Game 6 with confidence—knowing I had the Lord's power, love, and self-discipline. I trusted that He loved me no matter what happened. I pitched one of the best games of my life. I left the game in the seventh inning with a 5-0 lead. I didn't get a win, and neither did my team, but that night made me realize an important thing: That confidence I felt was all because of Jesus working in me. It's not about wins and losses. It's about how I did my job. It's about trusting God and what He gives us.

—RUSS ORTIZ

FOLLOW THROUGH

Do I live my life with fear and a continual worry of failure? Can I begin to trust the Lord to provide the tools necessary to compete?

For Further Reading: Get a copy of *Quiet Strength*, the Tony Dungy story, and begin reading it.

NO. 94 JESSE BARFIELD As a kid, Jesse would visit old Comiskey Park with his buddies and tell them: "I'm going to play here someday." Lots of kids say that. Jesse made it. In a 12-year American League career, Barfield smashed 241 home runs, won two Gold Gloves, and became an All-Star. In 1986, he led the AL with 40 home runs. "God will give you what He can trust you with," Barfield has said. And he gave this Chicago kid a dream come true.

95. WHAT HAVE YOU DONE FOR ME LATELY?

Strike Zone:
Worshiping an Unchanging God

*"The Lord is the everlasting God, the Creator
of the ends of the earth."*

Isaiah 40:28

Sports is a fickle business. We all knew that. But don't things seem a little more capricious in New York?

In October 2007, Joe Torre, a sure-fire Hall of Fame manager, rejected a half-hearted one-year offer to remain with the Yankees. His crime? New York's third-straight loss in the first round of the playoffs. Never mind the fact that Torre led the Yankees back to prominence during his 12-year tenure with an astounding 12 straight postseason appearances, including four World Series titles.

FAST FACT:

The Yankees won three straight World Series from 1998 through 2000.

But life in the Big Apple moves fast, and the Yankees didn't see fit to tie any more long-term knots with one of the winningest managers in baseball history. Torre moved on to manage the Los Angeles Dodgers.

Thankfully, we as Christians don't serve a fickle God. He doesn't change His mind, make rash decisions, or struggle with indecisiveness. He doesn't make mistakes or get caught by surprise. There's nothing in this world that causes Him to scratch His head and say, "Hmmm, didn't see *that* one coming."

Our God is eternal and unchanging. He is omnipotent, omniscient, and omnipresent—fancy words simply meaning that He is all-powerful, all-knowing, and exists everywhere. He is a God who "works out everything in conformity with the purpose of his will" (Ephesians 1:11). Moses described this aspect of God's nature most eloquently in Psalm 90:2 when he wrote, "Before the mountains were born or you brought forth the earth and the world, from everlasting to everlasting you are God."

What a joy it is to serve an unchanging, all-powerful God!

—JOSHUA COOLEY

FOLLOW THROUGH

How has God shown His faithfulness to you? Think, for instance, about where you would be without Christ and the Holy Spirit in your life. And think of how God's attributes bring you comfort and hope.

From the Playbook: Read Isaiah 40.

NO. 95 PAUL BYRD Randy Johnson has had his share of victims during his illustrious pitching career. Paul Byrd made sure he wasn't one of them. Byrd had pitched for the Mets and the Braves, but in August 1998, he was making his first start for Philadelphia. All he did was beat Johnson 4-0. Byrd went on to pitch for another 10-plus years in the majors, including several trips to the postseason. He told his story in the book *Free Byrd*, which details his life as a Christian in the world of baseball.

96. CHAOS OR VISION?

*"Where there is no revelation,
the people cast off restraint."*

PROVERBS 29:18

Chaos seems to be a theme nowadays. It seems that people's lives are in disarray. You can look at the covers of magazines at the grocery stores and see that chaos is a part of the lives of so many people. I believe this is a result of the lack of vision or a failure to trust in the vision God has given us in His Word.

FAST FACT:
Affeldt started 18 games for the Kansas City Royals in 2003.

No matter how successful or unsuccessful we are, if we don't have a reason for living we will never have an understanding of what path we should take in life. Without that reason or purpose, all we have left is chaos!

Once a person comes into the understanding that the reason he or she is here and is gifted with certain divinely disbursed talents is to glorify God, that person can finally escape chaos and live with vision ("revelation" is sometimes translated "vision" in this verse).

Our souls crave the Creator; our talents desire to make God smile. When God sees His creation doing everything possible to give Him credit for life and ability, people will begin to experience peace in their lives and homes.

Even when times are tough, those people who have vision and direction in the way God wants them to go and who understand what He wants them to become have a peace that surpasses all understanding (Philippians 4:7). That peace always rules out chaos.

Gain a vision for your life by trusting God's plan.

—JEREMY AFFELDT

FOLLOW THROUGH

What do you see as God's purpose for your life? Why has He given you the talents and gifts He has given? Are they to use for your own, personal glory or for His? How can you begin to use your talents in a way that fulfills God's vision for you?

From the Playbook: Read Philippians 4.

NO. 96 RAUL IBANEZ He could be among the best players you rarely heard of. Playing alongside the more famous Ichiro Suzuki in Seattle, Ibanez consistently knocked in 100 or more runs and hit 20 or more home runs for the Mariners. When he wasn't accumulating stats, Ibanez was reading—devouring faith-related books by Max Lucado and Lee Strobel.

97. HOW MUCH ARE YOU WORTH?

"While we were still sinners, Christ died for us."

ROMANS 5:8

A few years ago, when a certain baseball player signed a contract that would pay him eight million dollars a year (this was when that was an unusual amount of money), he unashamedly declared that he was worth that much. This guy was a good player, but most fans would disagree with his assessment of his value. It's hard for most of us to understand how anyone can feel he is worth that much money to hit and catch a ball for six months.

FAST FACT:

It is widely accepted that Nolan Ryan was the first baseball player to earn a million dollars a year. He signed a million-dollar contract in late 1979.

Yet there is one sense in which this rich outfielder really is worth eight million dollars—and more. But it's not because of his skills or his ability to draw fans to the ballpark. In fact, it has nothing to do with baseball.

His worth is because of the value God in His love places on each person—that guy included. When we consider the worth our God sees in us as His image-bearers—people for whom He sent Jesus to suffer and die, it's easy to see that we are worth at least eight million big ones.

We often estimate our value by how much money we make, by the cars we drive, by the house we live in, or by the titles we hold. Or we measure our value by the important things we do for others. Instead, we must realize that our value lies in the importance God places on us. And that value is based on two facts: God created us in His image (Genesis 1:27), and God loves us so much that He sent His Son Jesus to earth to die for us (Romans 5:8).

That makes your worth far exceed the contract figures of even the highest paid athlete. Because God sees your value through the sacrifice of His Son, you can't put a price tag on how much you are worth!

—DAVE BRANON

FOLLOW THROUGH

What makes you sometimes feel unworthy? Pause and think of Christ's sacrifice, and remind yourself of your value in light of what He did for you.

From the Playbook: Read Romans 8:31–39.

NO. 97 PHIL BRADLEY When his career ended in the majors, Bradley took his bat and went to Japan. His US batting average was .286, and he was an All-Star, but he felt that at age 31 it was time to move on. "We prayed that wherever we were sent, we'd go with a good attitude, trusting that God already had plans for us there." Bradley played for the Yomiuri Giants in Japan.

98. A GOOD NAME

"A good name is more desirable than great riches."
PROVERBS 22:1

D r. David Fletcher was standing at the spot where home plate once lay in Chicago's old Comiskey Park when he heard a voice. Fletcher claims the voice told him to contact Buck Weaver's family and work to clear the White Sox player's name.

Hey, I'm a baseball nut myself, but this is a bit much.

Weaver, for those of you under 137 years of age, played on the infamous 1919 "Black Sox" team that may have (probably!) intentionally lost the World Series against the Cincinnati Reds. Weaver claimed, quite plausibly, that he had played his hardest throughout the Series. But it was apparent that he knew about the scandal, and that was enough for baseball commissioner Kenesaw Mountain Landis to ban him from the major leagues.

Should Buck be reinstated? Dr. Fletcher and others think so.

FAST FACT:
Buck Weaver batted .324 in the 1919 World Series.

My guess is that if Buck Weaver could speak to us today, he might tell us about the value of a good name. It's a treasure that, once tarnished, is difficult to restore.

"Let love and faithfulness never leave you," says Proverbs, "Then you will win favor and a good name in the sight of God and man" (3:3–4). When the apostle Paul wrote to Timothy about the qualifications for a person serving in ministry, he stressed the importance of a good reputation "so that he will not fall into disgrace and into the devil's trap" (1 Timothy 3:7).

If we claim to be Jesus-followers, we must remember that sin in our lives will do damage to the cause (and the reputation) of Christ. Today, ask the Holy Spirit to guide your choices so that you will bring glory, not shame, to His name—and yours.

—TIM GUSTAFSON

FOLLOW THROUGH

Are your choices working for or against your good name? Are they protecting the holy name of God? What might Jesus think of your lifestyle decisions since it's His name that is connected to yours as a Christian?

From the Playbook: Read 1 Timothy 3:1–7.

NO. 98 TONY KUBEK Before there was Joe Morgan, there was Tony Kubek: player-turned-broadcaster. Wise and skilled, Kubek could analyze baseball as few men before or after. His playing career was relatively short (1957–1966—cut short by neck and back problems) but effective. He played in seven World Series with the Yankees, was a three-time All-Star, and was the 1957 Rookie of the Year. He spent 24 years doing NBC's Game of the Week back when that meant something. But after all that, he says, "The only reason we're here is to use our gifts to share the Word of God."

99. GOD IS GOD

"Be still, and know that I am God;
I will be exalted among the nations."

PSALM 46:10

The challenge was on! As we playfully talked trash back and forth, several of the pitchers from the Kansas City Royals suggested that I couldn't throw a baseball faster than 65 mph. *C'mon! You've got to be kidding me!* I thought. Granted, I never played collegiate or pro baseball—but in high school I was an All-Arizona player as a catcher. Surely I could break the 65-mph barrier! As we headed for the field one player, Ira Brown, grabbed the radar gun.

FAST FACT:
Released from KC, Ira Brown later played Division I basketball for the Gonzaga Bulldogs.

After throwing a few warm-up tosses, I headed for the hill to prove the guys wrong. I smiled, took a deep breath, wound up, and threw that baseball so hard I thought my arm was going to fall off! Snap! The ball hit the catcher's glove. As I confidently looked up at Ira, who was holding the gun, he shouted, "63 miles per hour!" I couldn't believe it! I was left humbly calibrated and in awe of the gift God had given these players who regularly pitched in the 90-mph range. The fact is, they were the pro baseball players, and I was not.

When it comes to God and us, it's the same way. I have to remember that God is God, and I am not. God is so powerful and so capable that I need to make sure to *not* get in the way of what He is trying to do in my life. The Bible says in Psalm

46:10, "Be still, and know that I am God; I will be exalted among the nations, I will be exalted in the earth."

Let God be in charge of every area of your life; allow Him to be Lord of your life. He knows a whole lot more about how to do that than we do!

—Travis Hearn

FOLLOW THROUGH

Are you a control freak? Do you try to control your own life? Maybe it's time to give God complete control and allow Him to rule your life.

From the Playbook: Read Proverbs 3:5–6.

NO. 99 BRIAN ROBERTS He's one of those guys who nobody would have ever guessed he'd become a major leaguer. Just 5' 9" tall, Roberts has had to convince people all along that he could do what he's done—which is make multiple All-Star teams, consistently hit for average, and be a team leader. At least twice, he led the league in doubles. One season he stole 50 bases. How did he do it? "I put my faith in the abilities God has given me. I rely on Him for everything."

Strike Zone:
Witnessing for Jesus

"If they keep quiet, the stones will cry out."

LUKE 19:40

One day as I was warming up for a game while playing for the Texas Rangers, a guy yelled down at me. "Hey, Curtis! We're glad you're a Ranger, but don't talk about Jesus."

I'd like to have a conversation with that guy. Here's what I would tell him:

"You see, I believe with all my heart that the Jesus of the Bible is exactly who He claimed to be: God in the flesh, the Jewish Messiah, and my own personal Lord and Savior. By no merit of my own, I was given an inheritance in an eternal kingdom called heaven."

Could anybody really expect me to keep my mouth shut when I have such good news?

On the first Palm Sunday, as Jesus was riding into Jerusalem, the people were shouting out to Him in praise. The Pharisees asked Jesus to make them stop for fear that they might stir up the Roman guard.

Jesus told them that if the people were to be quiet, then the rocks would cry out to praise Him.

Christian brothers and sisters, let's continue to keep the rocks silent by being Jesus' witnesses to all the earth. Are you seizing the opportunities that come your way to proclaim the truth?

FAST FACT:
After his 10-year major league career ended, Curtis graduated from Cornerstone University in Michigan with a degree in education.

Perhaps, though, you don't believe. Perhaps you say, "That guy is nuts." You can say that, but you can't say I don't care. It is my love and compassion for the human soul that urges me to share what I have found to be true.

You can call me a fool if you wish, but don't ask me to stop caring enough for you that I stop talking about the One who saves mankind.

—CHAD CURTIS

FOLLOW THROUGH

Who are two people who need to hear about Jesus? How can you tell them? Make it a point to do something about it this week.

From the Playbook: Read Matthew 28:16–20.

NO. 100 CHAD CURTIS In October 1999, Chad Curtis caught the last out of the twentieth century—ending the World Series won by his NY Yankees. Then he kept the ball and gave it to a friend as a thank you for something he had done for Curtis. By analogy, Curtis observed, "God was willing to give up something that He loved [Jesus] so He could do something for us." A no-nonsense guy who takes his faith seriously, Curtis parlayed his chance at baseball into a career highlighted by two World Series rings and more than 1,000 hits.

KEY VERSE LIST

BASEBALL PEOPLE

Brief biographical notes about the baseball people who contributed articles to Power Up!

JEREMY AFFELDT When Jeremy Affeldt was called on to pitch in the 2007 World Series, he did something unusual: He compiled an ERA of 0.00. Affeldt began his career with the Kansas City Royals in 2002. Affeldt is one of those rare pro athletes who attended a Christian high school.

MICHAEL BARRETT After beginning his major league career with the Montreal Expos, Barrett got a chance to play at Wrigley Field for over three seasons with the Chicago Cubs. His cousin Scott Fletcher had also played for the Cubs. In 2006, Barrett had his best season, hitting .307 with Chicago with 16 home runs.

SHAWN BOSKIE A first-round pick of the Chicago Cubs in 1986, Boskie spent four-plus seasons in the Windy City before starting a road tour of the MLB that took him to Philadelphia, Seattle, California, Baltimore, and Montreal. Boskie's best year was 1996 when he won 12 games for the Angels.

PAUL BYRD This is a man of humility. He understands that the fact that he has had a long and successful major league career is a surprise to many people—himself included. In 2008, in the middle of his thirteenth major league season, Byrd released his story in book form: *Free Byrd: The Power of a Liberated Life.* The 2008 season was the sixth time Byrd had won 10 or more games in a MLB campaign.

CHAD CURTIS When his 10-year major league career ended, Curtis didn't sit back, raise horses, and call it a life. He went back to college, earned his degree, and began a new career as a high school teacher and athletic director (and still raises horses). As an educator, he followed in the footsteps of his hero-father Ted, himself a teacher, and he put himself in position to challenge young people to a life of Christlike living.

MATT DIAZ Matt's appearance in this book gives us a mother-son writing tandem. Diaz grew up in Lakeland, Florida, where his dad, Ed, was the spring training chaplain for the Detroit Tigers. His mom, Gwen, is a successful freelance writer and public speaker. Diaz enjoyed a remarkable 2007 season as he established himself as a top hitter, batting .338 for the Atlanta Braves.

SCOTT FLETCHER It doesn't make you a superstar to be seventeeth in voting for the MVP Award. And it may not get you into the Hall of Fame to have Bill James call you the eighty-fifth best shortstop ever—but those things do indicate that Fletcher was a pretty good major leaguer. After being a first-round draft pick in 1979, Fletcher went on to accumulate 1,376 hits during his 15-year career with the Cubs, White Sox, Rangers, Brewers, Red Sox, and Tigers.

TRAVIS HEARN Okay, he's not a baseball person. In fact, although he did play some baseball as a kid, he's a basketball guy. Travis is the chaplain for the Phoenix Suns of the NBA. In addition, he's a nationally known motivational speaker, and he has even performed a hip-hop song to honor the NBA's Michael Redd.

BRYAN HICKERSON After a five-year career as a major league pitcher with the Giants, Cubs, and Rockies, Hickerson spent two seasons as a minor league pitching coach in the San Francisco system. But his true calling is in using baseball to reach others for Jesus Christ. That's why he joined Unlimited Potential, Inc. (UPI), an organization whose motto is "Serving Christ through Baseball." Hickerson's involvement with UPI has been focused on ministering to men and women in the military. He is also a chaplain for the Chicago White Sox.

MIKE MAROTH The guy who wrote *Why Bad Things Happen to Good People* could have used Mike Maroth as his prime example. Mike Maroth is a remarkable person. But in 2003, he suffered the pain of losing more than 20 games as a pitcher for the Detroit Tigers. Yet Maroth never once wavered in his faithfulness, his kindness, and his desire to help others. In fact, he and his wife Brooke received the 2004 Bill Emerson Good Samaritan Award for their philanthropic work through a group called Rock and Wrap It Up—which distributes food to the needy.

RUSS ORTIZ No matter what happens the rest of your life, if you could have one year like Russ Ortiz had in 2003, you've got a story to tell. During that season, Ortiz led the National League in victories with 21, he made the All-Star Game, his team made the playoffs, and he even hit two home runs. Before injuries started to diminish his effectiveness in 2005, Ortiz had fashioned a career won-lost mark of 103-60.

KARL PAYNE Like Travis Hearn, Karl Payne is not a baseball guy. He too is a chaplain, but he assists NFL players spiritually—not NBA players as does Hearn. Payne is chaplain for the Seattle Seahawks. Payne has served for many years as a pastor of youth at Antioch Bible Church, whose founder is Rev. Ken Hutcherson, a former NFL player.

BRANDON WEBB It didn't take long for Brandon Webb to establish himself as one of baseball's top pitchers. Kentucky-born righthander Brandon T. Webb won 10 games in his first season with the Arizona Diamondbacks, struggled through a 7-16 year in 2004, but went on to rack up nearly 70 wins in the next four seasons—two of which were Cy Young Award seasons ('06 and '08).

MICKEY WESTON This Flint, Michigan, native did something every kid baseball player dreams of doing: He made it to the majors. Sure, he had just one win on the mound and one save out of the bullpen, but who wouldn't love to live that dream? Weston pitched in parts of five major league seasons before retiring in 1993. Like Bryan Hickerson, Weston works with UPI, and he assists Hickerson in the chaplaincy for the Chicago White Sox

POWER UP WRITERS

Brief biographical notes about the writers who contributed articles to Power Up!

JEFF ARNOLD As a Chicago Cubs fan, Jeff Arnold probably doesn't get much support on that subject from his co-workers. Arnold is a writer for the *Ann Arbor News*, which is located not too far from Detroit and Comerica Park. Arnold covers a variety of sports for the *News*. For *Sports Spectrum*, he wrote articles about pitchers Nate Robertson and Mark Redman in addition to being a regular contributor for the *Power Up!* devotional guide.

ROB BENTZ After working for several years for *Sports Spectrum* magazine and radio right out of college, Rob attended Reformed Theological Seminary in Orlando, where he received a master's degree in ministry. He is now serving as pastor of small groups at a large church in Colorado Springs, Colorado.

DAVE BRANON For 18 years, Dave was managing editor of *Sports Spectrum* magazine. Currently, he is an editor for Discovery House Publishers and RBC Ministries. He is a regular contributing writer for *Our Daily Bread*. Over the years, he has written a number of sports-related books for a variety of publishers.

JOSH COOLEY A former writer for the *Baltimore Examiner*, Josh serves as a children's ministry administrator at his church in the Gaithersburg, Maryland, community. Cooley has written many articles for *Sports Spectrum,* including profiles of Scott Sanderson, Charlie Ward, and Brian Roberts.

DAN DEAL After working as a radio producer and occasional host of *Sports Spectrum* radio at RBC Ministries for several years, Deal left to work on the staff of Ada Bible Church in Ada, Michigan, as director of small group training and resources.

MART DE HAAN Mart is president of RBC Ministries. His grandfather, Dr. M. R. De Haan, founded RBC in 1938. Mart has written several books, including *Been Thinking About*, a publication of Discovery House Publishers.

GWEN DIAZ After she and her husband, Ed, completed a very important task—raising their four sons (one of whom is major league outfielder Matt Diaz), Gwen began to concentrate again on her writing career. Among her books are *The Adventures of Mighty Mom* and *Sticking Up for What Is Right: Answers to Moral Dilemmas Teenagers Face*.

TOM FELTEN Another former *Sports Spectrum* magazine person—Tom was manager of SS radio and magazine for several years—he now is managing editor of *Our Daily Journey*, one of the devotional guides produced by RBC Ministries.

TIM GUSTAFSON When not serving in the US Navy Reserves, Tim is managing editor of *Our Daily Bread*. He and his wife, Leisa, have nine children, just a few of whom have inherited Tim's love for the Detroit Tigers. Gustafson has served the Navy overseas in Japan and the Philippines.

BRIAN HETTINGA The host and producer of the weekly radio program *Discover the Word*, an outreach of RBC Ministries, Hettinga played small college basketball before trading in his Chuck Taylors for a microphone.

VICTOR LEE A former major league baseball beat writer, Victor left the notebook behind to serve as a pastor for single adults and evangelism at First Baptist Concord in Knoxville, Tennessee. One of his recent works is a book titled *Family to Family: Families Making a Difference*.

MARK MORAN Mark is a freelance writer who lives in Mesa, Arizona. He spends most of his time, however, as the news director of a Phoenix-area radio station.

JEFF OLSON When he has to put down his fishing gear or his hunting rifle and come inside, Jeff can be coaxed back to his desk at RBC Ministries, where he is a biblical counselor. Olson has written several booklets for the RBC Discovery Series of Bible studies. Besides his work with RBC, Olson has a counseling practice.

MOLLY RAMSEYER As a college student, Molly worked with *Sports Spectrum* magazine as an intern. She did such a good job she was offered the chance to write for the magazine later. After college, she began working with Youth for Christ on the local level. Currently, she is national director of camping for Youth for Christ. She lives in Englewood, California, with her husband, Dave.

ROXANNE ROBBINS After hobnobbing with the influential and famous in Washington, D. C., for several years in positions relating to public relations, Roxanne left it all behind to go to Uganda to live among kids with nothing. A longtime writer for *Sports Spectrum*, she knows athletes up-close and personal, but she has discovered the importance of the oft-neglected little guys and girls who cherish someone who cares for them.

RICK WEBER A correspondent for the *Houston Chronicle*, Weber has penned a few important articles for *Sports Spectrum*, including profiles about Morgan Ensberg, David Carr, and David Klingler.

NOTE TO THE READER

The publisher invites you to share your response to the message of this book by writing Discovery House Publishers, P.O. Box 3566, Grand Rapids, MI 49501, U.S.A. For information about other Discovery House books, music, videos, or DVDs, contact us at the same address or call 1-800-653-8333. Find us on the Internet at http://www.dhp.org/ or send e-mail to books@dhp.org.